CULTURE SHOCK!

Australia

Ilsa Sharp

·K·U·P·E·R·A·R·D·

In the same series

Britain	*Israel*	*South Africa*	*A Parent's Guide*
Burma	*Italy*	*Spain*	*A Student's Guide*
Canada	*Japan*	*Sri Lanka*	*A Traveller's Medical Guide*
China	*Korea*	*Switzerland*	*Working Holidays Abroad*
Denmark	*Malaysia*	*Syria*	
France	*Morocco*	*Taiwan*	
Germany	*Nepal*	*Thailand*	
Hong Kong	*Norway*	*Turkey*	
India	*Pakistan*	*USA*	
Indonesia	*Philippines*	*Vietnam*	
Ireland	*Singapore*		

Culture Shock! Australia
First published in Great Britain by
Kuperard (London) Ltd
No 7 Spectrum House
32-34 Gordon House Road
London NW5 1LP
1992

Revised 1994
Reprinted 1995, 1996

This edition for sale in Europe
(excluding the Netherlands)

© 1992 Ilsa Sharp

Illustrations by TRIGG
Photographs from Ilsa Sharp

Printed in Singapore

ISBN 1-85733-019-6

*This book is dedicated with respect and affection
to Australia,
a country which has had the foresight to welcome
the strangers knocking at her door,
and the courage to embark on an experiment
with multiculturalism.*

CONTENTS

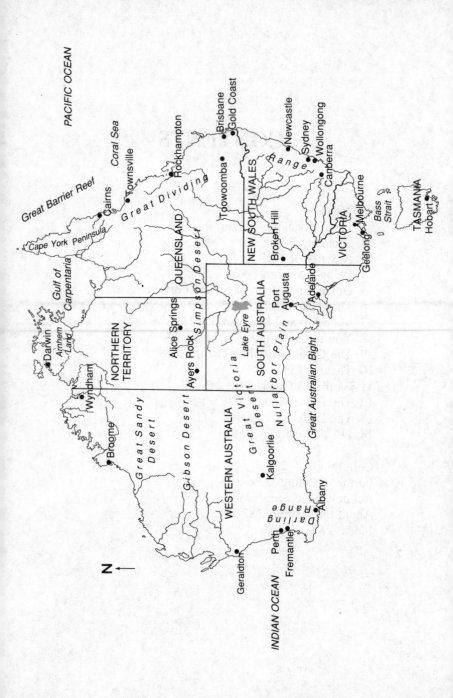

PREFACE

I would like to think that this book may help explain Australia to newcomers and visitors and thus bridge any 'culture gaps', improving the chances of mutual empathy and friendship. It is my particular, personal wish that Australia and Asia should draw closer together.

I hope too that the book will help Australians understand themselves and what it is that makes their culture unique, by holding a mirror up to them and asking them to see themselves through outsiders' eyes.

Finally, I must beg Australia's pardon if any of my interpretations have been skewed somewhat by my own 'Sandgroper' bias, due to being located at Perth, despite my best efforts to avoid such imbalance, and for any other inadvertent 'greenhorn' errors.

Chapter One

THE TYPICAL AUSTRALIAN

'He is a very nice fellow, certainly nobody would ever guess he was born in Australia.'

—British playwright and wit, George Bernard Shaw,
in his play *Major Barbara*, 1907.

Images, Stereotypes and Misconceptions

I can't count how many times my decision in the late 1980s to set up home in Australia, particularly Western Australia, was greeted with curling lips and an amazed 'But, why on earth would you want to live *there*?'

This told me more about the enquirer than about Australia.

Australia seems to be one of those countries that nobody feels neutral about. Everybody has strong views, for or against. Depending on where you are coming from then, geographically, psychologically and culturally speaking, you are sure to harbour in your heart one of a well-defined range of stereotypes depicting 'the typical Australian'.

So let's clear the air first by spelling out some of these stereotypes from the start. The most widespread, unfortunately, is 'The Ugly Australian', which seems to come in approximately three models:

European Model

If you are of continental European origin, this means the Aussie is barbaric, loud-mouthed, ignorant and uncultured, hopelessly provincial.

He is physically outsize but mentally minuscule, somewhat naive, and nearly always extremely badly dressed (this gaffe weighs particularly hard on the minds of the Parisian French). He cannot hold his wine, and has the temerity to claim that his own country produces this celestial ambrosia on a par with the French original. Worst of all, he cannot understand menus written in French. Basically, he is a peasant.

But actually, most Europeans are blissfully unaware of the existence of Australia or the Australians.

British Model

If you are British, you probably see your Antipodean cousin as a rather alarming, alien being bereft of the (hypocritical) courtesies of the mother country, far too frank (which other country could have produced a foreign minister who recently used the F... word in public while on an official tour of South Africa?), frequently obscene; a naive colonial boy in shorts, an insular sheep-farmer sporting a big hat with corks hanging off it to keep the flies away.

You find the way he tends to 'get physical' rather terrifying, although you secretly admire it too. And the way he puts himself on first-name terms with you from the word go is quite beyond the pale. He's notorious as a bloke fond of a booze-up, most often culminating in a 'technicolor yawn' or 'chunder' (in low Australian patois, a vomiting session)—which he performs in a back-garden 'dunny' (outshed toilet).

The Australian accent, furthermore, is execrable by British standards and unfortunately slots the Australian firmly into 'the lower classes', since it best resembles working-class Cockney from East End London, or Irish-dialect English.

Many of these British images derive from the Barry ('Bazza') McKenzie comic strip, which ran for years (1963–74) in the British satirical magazine *Private Eye*, lampooning the worst traits of an Aussie on the loose in Europe.

Asian Model

If you are Asian, you probably share the European and British concern at the Australian's admittedly blunt ways, since calling a spade a spade is hardly an Asian trademark. His predilection for semi-nakedness will not have endeared him to you, either.

And most likely, you have been persuaded that the typical Australian is a dyed-in-the-wool racist, besides being lazy or on the dole and totally incompetent because he can't seem to make as much money as you can—and even more irritatingly, for some reason, does not seem to *want* to make money, anyway.

He has no drive and to all intents and purposes, has parked himself in the world's KIV tray, his nation quite literally 'a basket case'.

Although it is true that where there is smoke, there usually are at least a few glowing coals, in fact, many of these images derive from a hostile Asian press, egged on by Asian governments intent on preventing their best and brightest from emigrating to Australia. (The Aussie media have, however, more than held their own, exchanging insult for insult, and then some.)

The culture gap is at its widest between Australia and Asia, a cause of enduring sadness to all concerned, for Asia is where Australia is located and where Australians eventually must, willy-nilly, make their psychological, cultural and economic home.

The Great Suburban Bore

A kind of sub-category within 'The Ugly Australian' classification is the Australian as 'The Great Suburban Bore'.

By definition, this view of the Australian can only be held by someone who thinks he himself or she herself is the opposite, i.e., sophisticated, intellectually dazzling, exciting, glamorous, etc. Well, we know what we think of people who think this of themselves, don't we? That would certainly be the Australian reaction to such pretentiousness, at any rate.

It is true that the vast majority of Australians lead simple lives, putting great store by their homes and families, and the general philosophy of *cultiver son jardin* (with the gardening bit taken quite literally). But then, what is so reprehensible about such simple values in our troubled times?

As chief Australia-watcher Professor Donald Horne, himself a native son, has said, describing Australia as the world's first 'suburban nation' in his seminal *The Lucky Country*, 'The profusion of life doesn't wither because people live in small brick houses with red tile roofs.'

Crocodile Dundee

Another, more positive, image of Australians bases itself on the 'Australian Pioneer' stereotype, one which many Australians themselves have taken to their bosom, along with sundry others, particularly the Americans. You can tell how much Aussies fancy

The goanna—diet of the Australian pioneer. Photo courtesy of the Northern Territory Tourist Commission.

themselves in this role by the number of them who don bush hats, cowboy hats or 'Digger'-style Aussie army hats, especially when showcasing themselves on trips abroad. Former labourer-turned-comic actor Paul Hogan's sell-out *Crocodile Dundee* films of 1985 and 1988 did much to fuel this myth.

This stereotype has it that every Australian is fit, tanned and courageous in the face of hideous adversities daily encountered in the bush and deserts of a harsh continent. He is attuned to the secret voice of Nature, thanks to his Aboriginal mentors, consumes goanna steaks most dinners and spends an awful lot of time fighting bush-fires, that is, when he's not locked in mortal combat with either crocodiles or lethally poisonous serpents. He is the original frontiersman (alias Davy Crockett) reborn.

Americans really relate to this myth, because many of them live its American counterpart, nursing the idea that they are all cowboys at heart, still conquering the Wild West.

A subdivision within the Australian Pioneer category falls into the *Rural Idyll* box: here, most Australians make their living herding

*Fitting into the landscape, the author on horseback in
the Avon Valley, Western Australia. Photo by Siva Choy.*

cattle or sheep, spending much of their time on horseback, bathed in
pastoral peace and romantic sunsets.

These fantasies of course completely ignore the fact that the
overwhelming majority of Australians—close to 90%—in reality
huddle together in urban centres, in mortal dread of the outback
beyond, terribly disturbed by the thought of having to deal with the
Aboriginals and blithely oblivious of their own burgeoning paunches.
If anything, the nearest they have ever got to the desert is burying
their heads in the metaphorical sand most of the time.

The Honey-Coloured Facts

As with all extreme stereotypes, the truth lies somewhere in between.

'The truth' is also changing rapidly, almost minute by minute, as Australia itself changes, under the impact of the geo-politics of the Australasian region, and of very varied immigration inflows, particularly from Asia.

How inadequate black-and-white statements are, about any country or culture! The truth in between is in fact not so much grey as honey-coloured when it comes to Australia: the country's distinguished first ambassador to China, Stephen Fitzgerald, has declared that this will be the national skin colour one day soon, thanks to Asian immigration and mixed marriages.

A fifth of Australia's 17.7 million people today were born outside Australia. By the middle of the 21st century, perhaps 20% may be of Asian origin. And this is not to forget the more than 200,000 original Australians—the Aboriginals.

Australia is no longer a bastion of white or Anglo-Saxon culture. The Anglo-Saxon foundations were in fact undermined long ago, with the influx of southern European immigrants after World War II, notably from Italy, Greece and Eastern European countries such as Yugoslavia. But as I shall explain shortly, the foundations cannot be ignored, even today.

Self-Image

What do Australians think of themselves? Fortunately, like their British ancestors, they are blessed with a limitless capacity for self-mockery, always a healthy trait. Home-bred intellectuals are at times far more critical than outsiders would be.

But one mocks only when the foundations are secure, and the fact is, the vast majority of Australians believe that their way of life is the best, and the right one. In fact, they are blissfully unaware that there could be any other way.

Their biggest failing, however, is that few of them realise just how lucky they are. They take their freedoms and the welfare system for granted, among other perks of the Australian way of life. For all their detestation of the 'whinger', they themselves are capable of whingeing about the most minute infringements of their rights. They need to travel more, to bring back sobering lessons from the tightly 'guided democracies' and outright dictatorships of the developing world.

Call it smugness and complacency if you will, but there is an attractive sense of security, pride and identity in the ordinary Australian's conviction that he has got it right.

The Cultural Cringe

The only chink in this armour is the famous 'Cultural Cringe'. This originates from an uncomfortable suspicion that anything British, from the original motherland, was *per se* better than homegrown Aussie stuff. In these post-British Empire days, there are now variations on this theme, focusing on Europe: I have met Australians who are obsequiously obsessed with the notion that anything French must automatically be superior, for instance.

I have met Australian diplomats, ostensibly charged with the job of promoting their country, who were only too eager over a private dinner table to dissociate themselves from what they saw as the unspeakable yobbos of their homeland.

This inferiority complex, which for a moment showed happy signs of diminishing during the 1970s, has revived with a vengeance now that a heavily indebted Australia is plainly in dire economic straits, particularly in comparison with its non-white neighbours, such as the 'Mini-Dragons' of Hong Kong, Taiwan, South Korea and Singapore.

This has led to extensive self-flagellation in public places. At the end of 1990, it was even announced that the Federal Government would sponsor annual lecture tours of Australia by disgruntled expatriate Australians, to give 'an objective viewpoint' of the nation.

Announced by the Federal Employment, Education and Training Minister, John Dawkins, these lectures are the brainchild of Professor Donald Horne. The lectures were to take place on Australia Day itself, usually a case for national celebration and self-congratulation.

'The Cringe', still a topic of eager discussion in the Australian press, learned works and the like, permeates Australian culture and indeed its economy (which is importing too many foreign goods for its own good, in preference to those made in Australia). There is still the lurking worry that Australian-produced cinema, literature and fashions—the whole gamut of creation—may not be as good as 'the real thing', from Hollywood, Britain or France.

The Colonial Past

Such discussions will ring a clangorous bell with other 'developing' nations who share Australia's colonial past—similar debates on the worth and universality or otherwise of local literature occur from time to time in Singapore and Malaysia, for example.

In short, he who wishes to understand the Australian mind, needs to study the country's history and to take both convict-hood and the 'colonial factor' into careful account.

The Australians who called England 'home' and valued a pukka British accent are still with us today, albeit dwindling in numbers and influence. The Queen of England is still the Queen of Australia, albeit perhaps not for too much longer, judging from the gathering momentum of the Republican movement in Australia.

Despite all the overlays deposited by post-World War II migration, the key to mainstream Australian culture still lies in the 19th century, working-class London and Ireland from which the first, convict, Australians were unwillingly torn—to the extent that you still hear forms of the English language in Australia which are no longer currency in modern England itself.

I would go so far as to say that a good way to understand Australia, especially for non-Europeans, might well be to spend a couple of years in London first. A tortuous route for some, perhaps, but a worthwhile soft landing, compared with going in cold.

In this context, I continually marvel at the bravery of the thousands of Asian and other non-English speaking migrants who every year struggle to bridge the enormous cultural and linguistic chasm separating them from 'the real Australia'. Without my own British background, I do not know how I could possibly have begun to understand Australia. But even a British grounding is still only a beginning.

The Battler

The typical Australian also invariably likes to see himself as that national icon, The Battler—a working-class underdog who struggles to survive, the salt of the earth. This is the model he emulates. Hence his odd celebration of a major military defeat like the Battle of Gallipoli in 1915, during World War I.

The Tall Poppy

However, should the battler actually win and come out on top, achieving success, fame and money, he immediately transforms into a Tall Poppy, a most undesirable thing, begging to be cut down to size. The typical Australian tries not to shine too obviously and does not much like those who do, although he also prides himself on his ability to give everyone 'a fair go'.

Street-Friendly

It is true that Australians have 'country ways' for the most part; this is a large part of their considerable charm. They take a direct, simple approach to things and people, can be quite child-like at times. Their most delightful characteristic is a willingness to talk to strangers in the street, on the bus, anywhere, and to spend time with you—they are rarely in a hurry. (This principle may not apply in the centre of Sydney at rush hour, however—capital cities will be capital cities.)

Singaporean journalist Chai Kim Wah nutshelled this quality neatly in an excellent travel report in the *Sunday Times* of Singapore, November 26, 1989: 'A trait I came across often (was) a readiness to give you the time of day, to be matey. It is not the American gushing-on-all-eight-cylinders friendliness, but a laid-back variety you can take or leave.'

Never be afraid to greet an Aussie in the street or to talk to a taxi-driver; always take the initiative if you can, because you will inevitably be rewarded with a smile and friendly conversation. This presupposes, of course, that you can speak English. Most Australians are not comfortable at all with foreign languages; and good English is still the *sine qua non* key to their hearts.

Mateship

Once your friend, the Australian is characteristically your friend for life, for better or for worse. Loyalty, 'mateship', still counts for much.

And there probably can be no better friend in a physical crisis than an Australian. The Australian somehow seems to revert to the 'Pioneer' stereotype at the sight of fires, floods or crime—he will always roll up his shirt-sleeves (or more typically, take his shirt off) and charge in to help, oblivious to his own personal safety.

I shall never forget how my Australian neighbours demonstrated this quality when a serious fire broke out in the wooden-hut village down my road in Singapore. By the time I got to the scene, having dithered around putting on the 'right' clothes and shoes, and then dousing myself in water first, the Aussies were already running in and out of the flames, stripped down to their underwear, carrying the villagers' sticks of furniture out of harm's way.

Proud and independent they may be—and they expect others to be likewise—but Australians do know how to band together in times of crisis and are always quick to lend a helping hand to their fellow man, a habit learned in the bad old days of bush settlement.

Asians, and others too, have often wrongly labelled the Australian 'individualistic'.

Mateship is what makes the difference even to the most conservative Australian. The same Australian who has just made disparaging remarks about Asians to white friends over the dinner table, will the next minute deck any white who insults the Asian friend and neighbour with whom he has been enjoying a pint of beer at the pub for the past few years—'cause mates are mates, see? He himself is unlikely to perceive the paradox.

Scout's Honour

The Australian can be naive—long may he stay that way. It is only yesterday that most, even in the cities, kept their front doors open to visitors and never locked their cars. All that has changed, but it is still all too easy to take advantage of the Australian's innocence. He takes you at your word, and expects it to be your word of honour too.

It seems inevitable, although lamentable, that the Australians will be pushed into the harsh real world. Already, it is not as easy as it was to walk into a bank and open an account in the name of Mickey Mouse without showing any identification whatsoever. But that, too, was only yesterday.

You can phone up and open a Telecom Australia account without any paperwork or further ado, sight unseen. You leave your passport at the Immigration office but get no receipt for it to prove that they have it. Why? Because this is a matter of trust between you two, right? You wonder if anyone else who asked for it could get it over the counter. But you are not supposed to worry about this, because it is all a matter of trust. Just as you are supposed not to worry when the passport comes back to you complete with your desired visa, but are you supposed to worry when you deposit a large amount of cash into a bank account and get no documentation to prove you have ever paid it in – no worries, the clerk is your mate, right, he/she would never dream of siphoning a bit off for himself/herself.

The two most famous Aussie catch-phrases, 'She'll be right,' and 'No worries' assume the essence of the Latin *mañana* or 'Oriental fatalism' at such times.

Naiveté is why Australians have had some trouble doing business in Asia. They are not used to hidden meanings behind words. As far as they are concerned, words mean exactly what they say.

This attitude hardly fits them for the arcane shadow-play of business in countries like Indonesia or China—no wonder Broken Hill Proprietary, or BHP, Australia's huge steel corporation, irritably announced its withdrawal from most China investments in April 1989, pronouncing itself thoroughly frustrated with 'a continuing series of negotiations and attempts at building and maintaining relationships'.

The Soft Underbelly

Lastly, I have observed that, contrary to the machismo pervading the nation's self-image, Australians are incredibly soppy sentimentalists. It's a short step from slap-on-the-back mateship to blubbering on each other's shoulders at the pub.

You have only to study the Australian creative style in film-making, whether for advertising or for the cinema, to be struck by its lingering, lyrical quality, its preference for tear-stained soft focus. (Those familiar with the famous 'Singapore Girl' advertisements patented by Singapore Airlines, which fit very much into this genre, might remember that the image-creator behind them is an Australian by adoption.)

The Australian's shell is rough and tough, a protection born of his violent past in a harsh land; but if handled sympathetically, he will turn turtle and show you his soft underbelly.

Chapter Two

SPEAKING STRINE

'To employ more than the most limited of vocabularies is not only ostentatious but anti-democratic. If the teachers are half right, little has changed since I attended primary school in the 1940s, when to show an interest in words was to damn yourself as some sort of deviant. As a wimp, or worse.'

—Columnist Phillip Adams in *The Weekend Australian*,
July 27, 1991, on the Australian attitude to words.

An English-speaking Country?

Nothing distinguishes the Australian more sharply from the average Anglo-Saxon than his very special brand of English.

Many English-speaking newcomers to the country make the awful mistake of imagining that operating there will be a breeze because 'They speak English there, don't they?' Well, not quite. Like English in other former colonial outposts, from the West Indies to South Africa and Zimbabwe, from India to Singapore and Malaysia, the language has mutated in Australia's desert soils.

The extraordinary thing is that many of the central features of Australian English were well in place by the late 19th century, hiving off from the mother-tongue very soon after the original convicts' and settlers' arrival in Australia. The language of a rebellious subculture.

Unfortunately, the lingo is extremely hard for the outsider to penetrate, or to imitate (Try saying 'Australia' the Strine way – 'Ors-TRY-ya'). If you are a new migrant, you may gain comfort (or despair, depending on your point of view) from the certain knowledge that your children will be fluent 'Strine' speakers within months of setting foot on Australian soil. ('Strine' is an approximation of how the word 'Australian' sounds, coming out of an Australian's mouth.) It's definitely catching.

There is still an older generation of Australians, particularly the more educated ones, which was brought up to speak 'English English', but this cohort is fast dwindling. There are also some distinctly well-moderated, gentler accents to be found among educated and well-travelled Australians, especially in the eastern states, in major cities such as Sydney, Melbourne and Adelaide.

Although the trend is definitely for a more earthy Australian accent to take over the airwaves, out of a sense of increasing national pride, there are still quite a few such moderated accents to be heard on 'Auntie', the Australian Broadcasting Corporation's radio programmes.

No Plums Please, We're Australian

Generally speaking, though, you will be considered suspect and a bit 'up yourself' (an obscene but commonly heard reference to sexual gratification of yourself; 'wanker' is another frequently heard insult of the same breeding, referring to masturbation) if your English comes with too 'plummy' an accent. ('Plummy' refers to the over-careful speech you would produce if you had a plum in your mouth.)

Not only does the majority of the nation favour 'Ozspeak' but there is now also a subgroup of youngsters whose dialect of choice is sarcastically alluded to by older journalists as 'Wayne-speak', this term being a reference to today's 'in' names for Australian children, Wayne (or Jason; female version, Bron), rather than the good old Bruce (or Jan). (There was also a brief hippy interlude during the 1960s, which produced Amber, Jasmine, and Sky for some.)

Much of Wayne-speak is plain old lousy pronunciation, rather than just dialect English. Examples are *heighth* for height and *esculator* for escalator, as noted by journalist Deborah Bogle in an article for *The Australian Magazine*. In the same category can be bagged the increasing tendency to pronounce 't' as 'd', thus, *qwordah* for quarter and *wor-dah* for water. Overlaid on this is the growing impact of American English.

Today or To Die?

True-blue Australian English differs from the 'mother-tongue' both in terms of its accent and in terms of its vocabulary. The accent is best gauged from old jokes which run thus ...

Wounded soldier to nurse in Australian hospital:

'Have I come here to die?'

Nurse: 'Now, love, yer came 'ere yesterdie!'

And a punning headline in *The West Australian* newspaper, 30 April 1993, would not have been possible were it not for the Aussie accent: referring to Princess Diana of England, the newspaper head-lined 'Diana—Princess of Wiles'.

... and the national form of greeting, 'G'day, mate!' (not common currency between the sexes or among women, it should be noted), which could be transcribed roughly as 'Ger-die, mite!' Woe indeed were my two migrant friends desperately looking for Hay Street—they would have been better understood if they had said 'High Street' like everybody else in Australia.

Be very careful whom you label an Australian on first hearing. It is difficult for the beginner to tell an Australian accent from a New Zealand one, but New Zealanders do not like to be taken for Australians, not one bit (the feeling is mutual). As a general guideline, Australians open their mouths wider, while New Zealanders are said to speak through their clenched teeth and semi-closed lips. Typically, a New Zealander will say 'yis' for 'yes', and 'fush n' chups' for 'fish and chips', somewhat like the Scots' accent.

The contortions that Australians can perform with diphthongs are a marvel to the ear. Often they are extended to double-diphthongs, to the point that a simple 'no' may well become more like 'nah-oh-oo-u'. For reasons I do not quite understand myself—probably sexist ones—the essentially nasal accent sits particularly uneasily with the female voice, which in Australia also seems to be higher-pitched than it would be in most of Western Europe (although not so much higher than is common among Asian females).

A commentator in the 1940s once surmised that the Australian accent was attributable to a permanent inflammation of the nose, due to the excessive pollen to be found in the air. Australian vocal delivery is most often slow and rather flat by outsiders' standards, without great light and shade contrasts, tending to a monotone in some cases. An Australian is capable of saying something extraordinarily interesting and lively in such a low-key manner that you may not notice he has said anything out of the way at all.

Ups and Downs

For this reason alone, never mind the accent, you need to concentrate on what Australians are saying (try hard not to fall asleep), in case you miss something. Since the Australian also has a penchant for terse understatement, the risk of misunderstanding is great.

Clearly, there is a corollary here to guide you on how you in turn should converse with an Australian. Loud, assertive delivery will not go down too well. Lower your voice and flatten it like his, erase all excitement or emotion, and you should be able to get your point across without too much offence.

There is one interesting exception to this rule: the infectious Australian habit of lifting the voice at the end of the sentence as if asking a question or seeking your approval/understanding.

'And it was raining, really *hard*' (on 'hard', the voice goes sharply up as if '?' were there and '... you know what I mean?' were tacked on the end), 'but we had no umbre*llas* ...' (up again on 'umbrellas' ... 'you know what I mean?').

This verbal tic can be infuriating to the novice but it will insidiously creep into your own voice over time, sure as the sun shines. And when you think about it, it is really quite a friendly habit, this constant seeking of your involvement in the conversation.

Antique Hangovers

Some Australian English is in fact more original and 'pure' than the version spoken in Mother England today. Many Australian words were long ago discarded in England. Australians as a rule betray their innate conservatism by clinging on to old forms and idioms, while at the same time building on top of them by creating new ones. This makes Australian English quite a rich, 'dense' language.

Again, you have to look back to white Australia's roots in 19th-century, Cockney London and Ireland to understand this. Quite apart from the accent, how else can you explain the extraordinary survival of Cockney rhyming slang in everyday Australian speech? It even gets printed in the daily newspapers as a matter of course— like the photo caption I once came across, reading 'Mr So-and-So on the dog and bone'. The photo in question showed Mr So-and-So using the telephone.

I might have passed this by and thought nothing of it, had not a young Aussie friend remarked to me over a coffee, 'So you're all on your Al Capone, then?' when I said my husband was away. That of course translated as 'So you're all on your own, then?'

I must mention here, however, that at least one reputable dictionary lists 'Al Capone' as the rhyming slang for telephone (and not 'dog and bone'), but 'Pat Malone' as the rhyming slang for 'alone', so I am not quite sure where this leaves us. But the examples I have cited have come from my first-hand experience.

Thinking Little

An Australian idiosyncrasy is the strange obsession with reducing any word possible to its diminutive form.

Hence 'postie' for the postman, and even 'U-ie' for a motorist's U-turn. This too is quite a catching disease and the longer you stay in Australia, the more you will find yourself slipping into the habit.

There is a similar group of words which has been shortened with '-o' at the end: 'reffo' for refugee, 'Freo' for the port of Fremantle in Western Australia, 'rego' for car-registration, 'journo' for journalist, 'muso' for musician, and so on.

Together, these two forms of diminutives are thought to number at least 200. This list is sure to be growing by the minute.

Conversation Smoothers

Then of course, there are the famous Australian catch-phrases, 'No worries' and 'She'll be right,' epitomising the nation's fabled plucky optimism and laid-back style. These are by no means clichés and are still in common use, although 'Not a problem' seems to be gaining ground. 'She'll be apples' (from the rhyming slang 'apples and spice' for 'nice'?) belongs to the same family of phrases.

However, it must be said that the trials of economic hard times have of late strained even the most sanguine of Aussies and such phrases increasingly have a hollow ring to them, belying the desperation beneath.

EW/2

Phillip Adams

Jest a bit of (pollie) punchline

'Pay our pollies les

By ANDY WILLIAMS

'Dob in a neighb plea in manhunt

By JIM POLLARD

FATHER'S DAY BRIEF SALE

HOLEPROOF UNDERDAKS
Australian made. All cotton. Were $4.85.
THIS WEEK

$3

CHECKOUT

d beat from all walks of life

(Clayton) cops an arresting insight

For hard up cook there's always (chook)

A (garbo) always remembers

Another, fairly newly-arrived, phrase in this conversation-lubricating category is 'There you go.' This crops up all over the place and if you use it skilfully, it will help you blend into the Australian background nicely. As a shop assistant hands over your change, she may well say pleasantly, 'There you go,' as may a waiter delivering your order.

The Art of Abuse

When it comes to insults, the Australian suddenly springs to life and abandons his laid-backness with a vengeance.

If you should happen to become the butt of his artistry in this department, try to take it all with a smile and a pinch of salt. Do not take it to heart. In Australia, you must always be a sport. Better still, once you have got the hang of things, give back as good as you get—it's expected, and accepted.

Australian English is particularly rich in invective (especially the obscene sexual variety), easily matching close rivals, such as Cantonese, for example. Four-letter swear-words are used like punctuations by the man-in-the-street and even by politicians in Parliament. 'Bloody' hardly raises an Australian eyebrow. There is much worse to come.

If you come from a genteel background, it is best you prepare yourself for this and train yourself not to hear it. There will be no avoiding it. (The most painful experience is when your children start picking it up.) Relegate it to wallpaper status, for that is all it really is—wallpaper. Those 'bad' words have lost their violence and their meaning in Australian English, through over-frequent use.

'Bastard' is one word that leads to great misunderstanding. Learn that in Australia, more often than not, it is used *affectionately*, very rarely as an insult. Only when it is applied to a 'Pommy', an Englishman, is it really meant to hurt. (There are many other terms of racist abuse, but I shall deal with these in another chapter.)

Paradoxically, however, such words as 'F...' are still considered fundamentally taboo in Australia, as elsewhere. It was only in 1985 that the Western Australian police charged the Sydney comedian Rodney Rude with obscenity for using the F... word to excess onstage (once every three minutes, during a 90-minute show).

Western Australia has been one of the last bastions of a once uniformly puritanical Australian culture, yet this case was dismissed in the end with the following rationale, to quote the *West Australian* newspaper of April 22, 1986: 'Used in combination with the word "off", the offending word was vulgar and quite impolite, but well understood and not necessarily obscene. The word's primary meaning was "to copulate" but more often than not it was used simply as a strong expletive, and repeated use had tended to lessen the impact.'

Punchy Politicians

The master of Australian invective without sole recourse to swear-words must surely be the recently re-elected Australian Labor Party (note confused spelling) government's Prime Minister, Paul Keating, although even he has stooped to berating his political opponents in public as 'Boxhead', 'Pig', 'Clown', 'Sleazebag' and so on.

'At least I'm doing this for the history books,' Keating once told an over-investigative journalist. 'You're only doing it for tomorrow's fish and chips.' (A reference to the traditional wrapping for fish and chips, old newspapers.) To a leftwing delegate at the New South Wales state ALP conference in 1982, he remarked, 'You could talk under wet cement.'

The ALP's Foreign Affairs and Trade Minister, Gareth Evans, has a reputation for foot-in-the-mouthers. Not only did he dismiss a local policeman as 'F...ing useless!' while on an official visit to South Africa in 1991, but he also used the F... word in Federal Parliament in 1990, the first to do so in 20 years, dutifully recorded by *Hansard*. But then, Evans was reported by Alan Attwood in *The Australian Magazine* to have said to a friend, 'F... it, I'm not going to stand around being diplomatic and nice to everyone. If people had been less diplomatic about Hitler, we would not have had the f...ing Second World War.'

That just about sums up the standard Australian attitude to excessive politeness: it is anathema in a truly democratic society. Being able to call a spade a bloody spade is a politically important Australian freedom.

As for the Silver Bodgie himself (see Glossary), former Labor Prime Minister Bob Hawke is well known for once turning aside from the heckling of an old-age pensioner to remark *sotto voce*, 'Silly old bugger!' The remark was unfortunately overheard by the entire nation, courtesy of TV and radio.

With leaders like these using lingo like this, the man-in-the-street needs little further encouragement. After an upbringing soaked in English hypocrisy and a young adulthood saturated with Asian evasiveness, I personally have found this trait refreshing, once you get over the initial shock.

In the same vein, Australians have concocted some extraordinary and often ingeniously insulting similes, making hyperbole a typically Australian vehicle. 'Three old ladies dressed like Queen Elizabeth II in floral prints and sensible shoes tell me they think their premier Bob Hawke is as "shady as a rat with a parasol",' reported Singaporean journalist Chai Kim Wah in the *Sunday Times* of Singapore, November 26, 1989.

The simile is a dynamic living form. Of very recent coinage is one I myself heard: 'Yeah, he's as busy as a bricklayer in Beirut!' Then there is 'He's as camp as a row of circus tents!' referring to a person's gay tendencies. 'This idea hasn't got a snowflake's chance in hell!' is a popular one rigt now. More on the scatological side is 'That's not worth a fart in a hurricane.'

Mis-Speak

Differences in vocabulary can sometimes lead to hilarious misunderstandings, or embarrassing double-entendres. Take, for example, the experience of my Malaysian-Eurasian friend, a fresh migrant to Australia. Invited by some new Australian friends to their dinner party, she asked politely if she should bring anything along and was at first puzzled by their response: 'Yes, bring along a plate, will you?' Poor things, she thought, they must be a bit short of crockery, and so she took along practically her entire dinner service, only to discover that a 'plate' referred to a dish of cooked food. This was what is known elsewhere as a 'pot-luck' dinner, where each guest brings a contribution of food, a very common variation on the 'Bring Your Own' or BYO theme in Australian life.

And then there was my other Malaysian friend, a timid new migrant in his early teens. He had made arrangements to meet someone on a particular street and so he was loitering there quite peaceably at the appointed time until he noticed a large sign which said, 'No Standing At Any Time'. Panicked, he proceeded to pace up and down wildly in the belief that so long as he kept moving, he would not be arrested. But this was in fact a traffic sign, which in other countries would probably have read something like 'No Parking' or 'No Waiting'.

The Tender Tea-Trap

The classic in this genre is, of course, the Australian 'Tea'. The worst case scenario is that you, an English or Asian migrant, have invited your Australian friend round for Tea. The Australian will wait around hopefully—and hungrily—for a long time before he or she realises that 'Tea' is just tea, and very little more.

For an Australian, Tea is the full evening meal, known to most other cultures as 'Dinner'. Beware of 'The Tea Trap'—it still catches out many a foreign visitor!

Subcultures as well as communities within multicultural Australia have spawned their own lexicons. The surfing subculture is one example: when they refer to 'a Margaret' in Western Australia, they mean a big wave of the type found around the popular surfing beaches of Margaret River in southwestern Australia.

A Beer is a Beer is a Beer?

Besides the macro-differences between Australian English in general and other 'Englishes', there are also inter-state micro-differences to be considered.

In Tasmania, you can have a Jimmy (a beer) but elsewhere you would probably just ask for a Stubby (a small beer-bottle holding 375 millilitres). If in Western Australia, you ask for a Middy measure of beer, you will get seven ounces, whereas in New South Wales, the same order would bring you 10 ounces. In New South Wales, a Schooner will bring you 15 ounces of beer, but in South Australia, only nine ounces. And so on, *ad nauseam* ...

A pint, thank goodness, is just that.

As you can see, Australians take their beer ('grog' is the more authentically Australian word) very seriously indeed, and you will have to, too.

Budgies are Black

Input from ancient Aboriginal cultures, not to mention many newer migrant, minority cultures, has further complicated Australian vocabulary. Experts say the state with the heaviest intake of Aboriginal words is Western Australia—words like 'monaych' for policeman, 'nyunga' for an Aboriginal and 'wongi' for an Aboriginal from the goldfields area around Kalgoorlie. But you are unlikely to hear such words used in the city of Perth itself.

Few non-Australians realise that words as universally adopted as 'budgerigar' and 'kangaroo' are in fact Aboriginal.

Spelling Bee Damned?

The language is of course evolving, like any other living language. But that does not seem to be sufficient excuse for the sheer volume of misspellings on show in Australia.

I was charmed by the offer of 'Lovely Cheeries' outside a grocery shop and intrigued by the display of 'Laces and Brades' at a drapery shop. It was fascinating to learn in a leading television and entertainment magazine that the popular TV compere John Mangos has a beautiful 'Frency Penny' tree in his garden, but surely, this must have been a Frangipani?

Semi-literate shop signs and the like could perhaps be excused in the context of a multicultural nation full of non-English speakers. But what really is disturbing is the fact that very few official letters, from professionals and civil servants, manage to conclude without committing at least one—but usually far more—serious spelling mistake.

Add to this, uncertainty throughout the country as to whether to adopt English or American spelling and the whole situation spells, as it were, confusion. Even the ruling party of the 1980s–90s, the ALP, spells itself the Australian Labor Party, rather than using the English 'Labour'.

Joke for Democracy

Language, of course, is the foundation of any nation's sense of humour. And Australia's humour is special indeed. It is considered a sacred cow of sorts.

Significantly, when certain states decided in 1989 to legislate against public incitement of racial hatred, racial jokes were specifically excluded from the list of offences that could be penalised under the new laws. It is an article of faith in Australia that everybody must be able to take a joke. The freedom to pull tails, tweak noses and generally satirise all comers is considered fundamental to democracy. Probably the most internationally known of Australia's satirists is Barry Humphries, who has dissected Australian society far more cruelly than any outsider.

A great deal of non-satirical Australian humour is outrageous in some way, whether salacious or sacrilegious. There is almost nothing you cannot make fun of, from cripples to Christ on the Cross. Nothing is sacred, except the right to poke fun itself.

Catch comic acts like the 'Doug Anthony All-Stars' on TV (on 'The Big Gig', for example) or live, and experience this for yourself. It is typical of the quirky Australian sense of humour that this trio of daring young men is for no good reason named after a retired former leader of the ultra-conservative National Party, Douglas Anthony.

Australian humour is above all as dry as the country itself, always understated, and if possible, mumbled out of the corner of the mouth. Listen carefully—there are some gems around.

Your Verbal Camouflage

Finally, a word of advice to those trying to acquire Australian camouflage: do not rush in too enthusiastically greeting everyone 'G'day, mate!' This phrase is so quintessentially Australian that if you don't have a 'full-on' accent, to use another Australianism (and if you also look a little strange saying it, like, say, you are Chinese by race), you cannot really pull it off.

A useful greeting, more easily adopted by foreigners than 'G'day,' is 'How're yer going?' (frequently followed by the rhetorical 'Orright?'). On the other hand, the phrase 'No worries' is quickly and effortlessly adopted by most new arrivals, with some success. Also, the casual dropping here and there of single words, such as 'rego', 'dag' or phrases such as 'Good on yer!' (to indicate approval) can be achieved quite naturally.

To help you along the road, here's a brief, selected glossary of the most commonly encountered or the best-known Australian-English words.

GLOSSARY

Arvo Afternoon. 'See you this arvo.'

Bananalander A native of Queensland state, referring to its lush tropical botany.

Barbie The barbecue pit in your back garden, the centre of all social action during the Australian summer. Barbies are also barbecue parties serving charcoal-cooked meats and salads, always in the open air.

Bathers Bathing costume, swimming costume.

Battler A quintessentially Aussie concept, fronting a philosophy of life. The battler is the little man, the underdog struggling to survive, often in conflict with the top dog.

Beaut Great! Also common is 'Beauty!', pronounced 'Bewdy!'

Bickies Bucks, money. 'I reckon I could earn big bickies on this deal, mate.'

Bludger Usually used in the term 'dole-bludger'. A bludger is anyone who sponges off anyone else, someone who never buys his round of drinks, and in the case of dole-bludging, someone living off the state's unemployment benefits.

Blue A quarrel, a row, or else, a blunder.

Bodgie The Australian equivalent of a Teddy Boy in the 1950s. Former Prime Minister Bob Hawke has been dubbed 'The Silver Bodgie' for looking like a leftover Teddy Boy at times earlier in his political career, complete with loud jackets and sideburns, albeit silvering ones.

Bonzer Like 'cobber' (see below), this is another word which outsiders think is quintessential Strine but it too is obsolete now. It used to mean 'excellent'.

Bucketing To get or 'cop' a bucketing, is to be reviled, strongly criticised. The phrase recalls the pre-flush toilet days when human excreta were collected in buckets; in other words, when you get 'bucketed', you get a bucket of shit poured over you.

Buckley's Chance No chance. Origins of this phrase are obscure, but certainly of early 19th century date and Buckley clearly was a very unlucky man. This is also used more concisely, as 'You've got Buckley's of winning this bet, mate!'

Chook A chicken.

Chunder To vomit, the word deriving from a warning on board ship to those unfortunates happening to stand below the sea-sick, 'Watch under!' Fans of the Australian pop group Men At Work will remember that the word appears in the lyrics of their hit song,

The Land Down-Under.

Cobber Fondly believed by many to be one of the most typical Aussie slang words, referring to a friend, this word is in fact just about dead in the Australian dialect and would sound quite odd in today's conversation.

Cocky Originally, a smallholder farmer (mind you, 'small' is not so small in a big country like Australia), but used even of larger farmers now. From the smallholder's propensity to grow crops, only to have them eaten up by pest cockatoos.

Crook Sick or ill, badly done or formed, not right.

Crust Your bread and butter, livelihood. The question 'What does he do for a crust?' is quite common.

Dag Derogatory. A dag (the word being derived from the filthy matted wool at the hind end of a sheep) is someone who's awful in some way, whether badly dressed, pretentious or boring.

Daks/Strides Men's trousers. 'Daks' originates from a brand-name.

Dingbat A weirdo, someone eccentric or deranged.

Dinkum Most famously used in the fuller expression 'Fair dinkum', meaning 'Honest, it's the truth!' It refers to the 'real thing.' 'Dinky-di' is a more intense version of this.

Dob In To inform on someone, to betray, especially a friend, workmate or neighbour. The Australian Police recently ran a 'Dob In' campaign inviting citizens to use a hot-line phone number to report on anything suggesting drug consumption or dealing among their neighbours. Dobbing in for whatever reason, however, is not considered admirable behaviour in the Australian value system.

Drongo A hopeless loser, a stupid or clumsy person. After a horse in the 1920s which persistently failed to win a single race.

Drum Information, the latest news, the inside story. 'Hey, give me the drum on this stockmarket scandal, will you, Fred?' 'What's the drum on that takeover proposal, Pete?'

Dunny A legendary item of Australiana, the outdoors W.C. (toilet, lavatory) shed, pretty rarely encountered in cities nowadays, but in the countryside, still, anything goes.

Esky Portable cooling box used to carry food and drink (more importantly, beer) to picnics on the beach or in the park, etc. Derived from the original trade-name, 'Eskimo'.

Full Bottle Fully informed, well up in. 'Henry's not full bottle on this issue, so let's call Reggie instead.'

Furphy A rumour or false report. It arose from soldiers' tall-tale telling while sitting around water-carts (servicing the latrines) branded with the manufacturer's name, 'Furphy'.

Globe Where other English-speakers might buy a bulb or a light-bulb, Aussies always ask for a 'globe'.

Gong Medal or badge of authority. 'He looked important alright, all covered in gongs, he was.'

Good Oil All the latest news, the gossip, the low-down.

Grog Booze, liquor. Any alcoholic drink, but usually beer.

Gutser Come a gutser, meaning to come a cropper, to fail dramatically.

Jackaroo/Jackeroo Usually a young man working on a sheep or cattle station in the rough outback to get first-hand experience of farming. Typically, the jackeroo is a youngster from the city out for adventure or an apprentice with good connections who will later become a station manager. A jackeroo's life is almost synonymous with toughing it out.

Jammies Pyjamas (Pajamas).

Lakkies Rubber bands (from 'elastics').

Larrikin A rowdy no-gooder, a hooligan, a mischievous youth, a trouble-maker. But also a scallywag with a golden heart.

Lolly/Lollies An abbreviation from 'Lollipop'. In Australia this no longer refers only to iced confections on sticks which you lick, as it would in England, it means any sweet or candy at all, especially brightly coloured ones.

Nong A fool or simpleton.

Ocker The ultimate, uncultured Australian boor. He is almost certain to be found wearing shorts and thongs, as the Aussies call what others call flip-flops, Japanese sandals, etc, and clutching a can of beer over a protruding belly. He is also characteristically jingoistic and insular when confronted with other races, creeds or cultures or indeed, any culture at all. Thankfully, his tribe is dwindling very fast.

Pokey Poker machines, or more rarely, a jail.

Poofter A derogatory term for male homosexuals, very commonly used, probably to reaffirm what Australian men see as their central macho identity.

Pooh Shit. 'Oh, the cat's just done a pooh on the carpet,' or 'Oh dear, looks like I'm in the pooh with my boss again!'

Rage This has very recently acquired the meaning of 'to party wildly'. Hence, an all-night rock-video TV programme on Saturdays is titled *Rage*. You may well be invited to 'go rageing' at the weekend; do not be alarmed, this is probably an invitation to visit a few discos. It may have its origins in a farming term referring to over-excited cattle.

Ratbag An eccentric or stupid person. Gradually coming to have a very general derogatory meaning.

Ringer An outstanding performer. Originally the best shearer in the sheep-shearing shed. But in northern Australia, it usually only refers to a cattle muster.

Ripper Similar to 'beaut', this means 'terrific!' 'What a ripper night we had!'

Roo-bar A large and solid structure made of metal bars attached to the front of Australian cars. Any car driving out of the city needs this fixture to cope with kangaroos bounding into the headlights on country roads at twilight or night. A collision with a kangaroo will otherwise result in far more serious damage to you and your car than to the 'roo itself!

Root A dangerous one for Americans, this one. Americans may use it to mean cheering on their favourite sports team—'I was

The roo-bar to cope with kangaroos on roads. Photo by Siva Choy.

rooting for the Mets'—but in Strine it refers only to sexual inter-course, being the equivalent of 'screw'. You have been warned.

Rort What the Americans and British know as a 'scam'—a fraudulent scheme or stunt.

Sandgropers Natives of Western Australia, because their state is largely desert sand.

Shout Both a noun and a verb. A shout is a round of drinks, for which someone has to pay. 'When my shout came round, I did the honours. But the whole evening, he never shouted one drink!'

Smoko Short for a 'smoke', it has come to mean all features of a break from work, for a smoke, for tea and sandwiches.

Sticky Beak A graphic word for the nosey parker, he or she who sticks his or her nose into things. It can also be used as a verb.

Stubby When not a small beer-bottle, a pair of tight, short shorts for men. Rarely an attractive sight.

Swag In the past, the ill-gotten goods carried by a thief or vaga-bond, but today used of any traveller's quite legitimate bags and baggage. 'Here, you can rest your swag here while you come inside.'

Tart This sounds most offensive to English ears, since in modern English outside of Australia, it would normally refer only to a prostitute. But in Australia, it just refers to any young, and usually pretty, woman. 'Eh, that new tart he's dating is a bit of alright!' It is actually a contraction of the affectionate 'sweetheart'.

Technicolor Yawn Coined by Barry Humphries' comic-strip anti-hero, Barry McKenzie, this lurid phrase refers to a particularly violent bout of throwing-up, usually induced by an excessive intake of alcohol.

Tube A can of beer, another word popularised by the Barry McKenzie comic strip of the 1970s.

Tucker Food. 'Bush tucker', for example, refers to the berries, roots and wild animals (lizards and the like) that you would have to eat if living off the land.

Two-up A traditional Australian gambling game based on spinning two coins and betting whether they will fall as two heads or two tails. A two-up gambling den is often referred to as a 'Two-up School', but even Australia's most respectable casinos feature this game, which originated in the pioneer outback.

Wag To skip something, drop out or play truant. 'My daughter's been wagging school for weeks, the head-teacher just told me.'

Whinger Anyone who complains too much instead of getting on stoically with being a battler like the rest of Australia. 'Poms'—the British—are supposed by Australians to have developed whingeing into a fine art.

Wowser A killjoy, one who lectures, a puritan. The wowsers would like everything to close up on Sundays again, just like the old days in Australia (not so very long ago)—no Sunday shopping, no Sunday drinking, etc.

Yakker Not to be confused with 'yacker' (a talker), this word means 'work'. 'Did a bit of hard yakker in the garden the other day, pulled my back, mate.'

Yard A general term used for the land at the back of your house, whether it is in fact a garden or a paved area.

Youse Probably of Irish origin, substitutes for 'you'. 'Youse blokes is OK,' or 'One of youse, come over here.'

Some Idiomatic Phrases

I'll give it a go; I'll give it a burl.
I'll try, never mind if it doesn't work, but I'm sure it will ... This mindset, while optimistic, can however lead to amateurism when it comes to the more precise technologies.

I suppose it's better than a poke in the eye with a burnt stick.
It's better than nothing. Again, this sums up the dryly humorous Australian approach in ordinary conversation. As *The Bulletin* weekly magazine put it in 1974, this is the Australian way of expressing ecstasy. The answer to a question like 'I've just won the Lotto for a million bucks, whaddya think of that?' could well be 'S'alright ...'

If it was raining palaces, I'd get hit on the head by the dunny door.
I never have any luck.

Don't come the raw prawn with me.
Don't try to bluff me, to put one over me.

Good on yer!
Good for you, well done!

In like Flynn
To seize an opportunity with enthusiasm, especially a sexual one. It derives from the energetic romantic exploits of the Australian-born (Tasmanian) Hollywood hero of 1930s movies, Errol Flynn. An example of how Australians cling on lovingly to phrases long out of date, this one is still in common use—'Oh, what, a picnic on the beach? Sure, he'll be in like Flynn for that.'

I'll be in that; I'm up for that.
I'm pretty keen to do that, alright.

Some Common Aboriginal Words

Billabong A waterhole.

Boomerang The curved Aboriginal hunting weapon that returns to its owner after hitting its target, making sophisticated use of aerodynamics.

Corroboree A festive gathering, a get-together, usually with music and dance.

Humpy An Aboriginal bark hut, now any rough hut or shelter.

Walkabout The habit ingrained in Aboriginal culture, of temporary migration from one's home base, for an unplanned period of time and often without a specific goal in mind. Used now of anyone who disappears mysteriously for a while to be alone or to escape something. 'Can't find Bill anywhere, musta gone walkabout.'

Some Common Diminutives

Brickie Bricklayer.

Chrissie Christmas.

Cozzie Swimming costume.

Deli Delicatessen shop or counter.

Divvie Dividend.

Footy, Footie Australian Rules Football.

Pokie Poker machines, in casinos, etc.

Prezzie Present, gift.

Sickie Taking sick leave off work. Often used jokingly, on the understanding that it is just a way of getting off work. 'Your party's on Thursday morning? No worries, I'll just take a sickie and I'll be there.'

Tazzie Tasmania.

Tinny A tin-can of beer.

Uni Where others might say 'varsity' (antique British) or 'U', the Aussies say 'Uni' for University.

Selected Rhyming Slang

Bag of Fruit Suit.

Butcher's For Butcher's Hook = Look ('I'll just take a butcher's at the baby for a minute').

Chevy Chase Face. (An interesting potential source of confusion for Americans, this one, as a well-known comic film actor in the USA is also named Chevy Chase.)

Dog and Bone Telephone.

Khyber Pass Arse.

Plates For Plates of Meat = Feet.

Pot For Pot and Pan = Old Man = Dad.

Steak and Kidney Sydney.

Titfer For Tit for Tat = Hat.

Trouble and Strife Wife.

Selected Acronyms

ACT Australian Capital Territory, the territory of the Federal Government, in which is situated the city of Canberra, the seat of Federal Government.

ACTU The Australian Council of Trade Unions, a power in the land.

AJA Australian Journalists' Association.

ALP Australian Labor Party.

ANZAC Australian and New Zealand Army Corps. A word to conjure myths of the Australian warrior with, a word endowed with great sanctity, referring to war heroes and martyrs, particularly during World War I and to some extent, World War II as well.

ASIO Australian Security Intelligence Organisation, Australia's official intelligence outfit (like the British MI5 and American CIA, etc.)

RAAF Royal Australian Airforce.

RAN Royal Australian Navy.

RSI Repetitive Strain Injury, a topic of some controversy recently, as workers have claimed compensation, sick leave, etc. based on this malady. Some doubt whether it exists, but it refers to the damage done by very fast hand and arm work in repetitive patterns, particularly as performed by computer keyboard operators and typists.

RSL Returned Services League, an ex-servicemen's association, synonymous with crusty old conservatives, usually anti-migrant and anti- just about everything about New Australia.

RSPCA Royal Society for the Prevention of Cruelty to Animals.

SBS The Special Broadcasting Service, established in 1977, which runs programme material by, for and about ethnic minorities in Australia. SBS TV has in fact gained acclaim beyond the minority communities for its excellent coverage of foreign news and enlightened programming, including good foreign feature films and documentaries. It features newsreaders and presenters of non-white and non-Anglo Saxon origin, even if they have foreign accents.

TLC Not exclusively Australian, this one, but I have noticed many Asians struggling with it. It's short for 'Tender Loving Care'. When your friend's little Billy has got a bad flu, you might remark, 'Oh, I'm sure he'll get well soon with a bit of TLC from you!'

Chapter Three

A SENSE OF NATION

'For many Australians, Asia is still a continent to fly over on the way to London. This will slowly change, especially now that the study of Asian languages has been made a school priority. Tomorrow's Australian will be proud of his European cultural heritage but is less likely to be white and will be much more appreciative of the cultures of Asia.'

—New Year editorial in *The Weekend Australian*,
December 30, 1989.

Australians know how to laugh at themselves, as I have said. But try laughing *at* them as an outsider and you will find the ground rules have suddenly shifted beneath your feet. Such sensitivity is not unusual in young nations—and white Australia's 200 years or so *is* still young in the history of nations.

Get Wise about Gallipoli

I have said that anything is fair game when it comes to Australian humour: from cripples to Christ on the Cross. This is true. But not Gallipoli …

Gallipoli? You will certainly have to get wise about Gallipoli if you wish to penetrate the Australian psyche. Anyway, you only have to stay long enough in Australia to hit the Anzac Day national holiday on April 25 to understand its importance.

No matter how small the Australian town you may chance upon on April 25, you can be sure there will be an Anzac Day parade around the local war memorial, complete with emotional speeches, brass bands and little boys clutching their fathers' hands, both wearing the traditional cocked Digger slouch hat. ('Digger' has been the name for an Aussie soldier since World War I, but nobody seems to know for sure why, possibly because so many Aussies are miners of Australia's considerable mineral resources, including gold.)

Gallipoli was the site of a great battle during World War I, in Turkey. The only thing is, like Dunkirk, France, in World War II, it was a great defeat and retreat, not a great victory.

The British, who still remember the evacuation from the beaches of Dunkirk with pride, and perhaps the Americans, who similarly still remember non-victories like Custer's Last Stand against the Sioux Indians in the 19th century or MacArthur's retreat from the Philippines during World War II, may perhaps empathise with the Australian celebration of failure at Gallipoli.

For others, particularly 'face'-conscious Asians, it may take a little longer to get the hang of things. You may as well hear the whole story now, from me. It will save you some mystification later, when the great April 25 fuss hits you via the newspapers, television and radio. As columnist Max Harris has commented in *The Weekend Australian*: 'Australians regard an honestly won failure as the essence of success. We're a weird mob.'

Anzac Day commemorates the terrible trials of the Anzacs—the Australian and New Zealand Army Corps—in their attempts to scale and control the rugged sea-cliffs at Gallipoli, from the landing date, April 25, 1915, until their withdrawal on December 19 that year. During this time, 8000 or so Australians (and more than 2000 New Zealanders, as well as French soldiers and others) were killed, and 19,000 Australians were wounded. Their bravery in the face of hopeless odds won the Australian soldier an enduring reputation thereafter, to this day—one reconfirmed elsewhere, as at the battle for Singapore in 1942.

The real significance of Gallipoli lies not so much in the nobility of the Australians' dogged courage in attempting the almost impossible, nor in their legendary 'mateship' unto death, but rather in the fact that they were fighting for, and obeying orders from, the imperial British government. This despite the fact that Australia had announced its intention to become independent of Great Britain in 1900 and had proclaimed the Commonwealth of Australia in 1901, holding the first federal elections that same year.

The sense of abandonment experienced at Gallipoli—it was all British war leader Winston Churchill's fault—saw the beginning of the end for Australian ties with the 'mother country', Britain. Australian director Peter Weir's epic film of 1981, *Gallipoli*, conveys this well; find a video of it if you can.

Underlying the Gallipoli celebration each year then (including the wheeling out still of octogenarian and nonagenarian survivors), is not anti-Turkish feelings (on the contrary, the fashion nowadays is for survivors of both sides to embrace one another), but strong anti-British sentiment, and a feeling of 'To hell with all the others.'

The historic animosity for the British felt by the Irish, who formed a large part of Australia's original convict settlers, has reinforced this feeling. (Britons, beware of telling your favourite Irish joke in Australia before you ascertain your host's family origins.) Gallipoli crystallised a sense of nation; hence its sacred-cow status when it comes to acceptable jokes.

The moral of the story: do not poke fun at Gallipoli and, despite his cultural ties with England, do not imagine that the Australian is just an Englishman in disguise. He is his own person. For one thing, he has learned to cope with a country about 24 times the size of the British Isles.

Breaking from Britain

Yet it is only recently that Australia has broken free of the British sphere of influence.

Although the federated Commonwealth of Australia was proclaimed in 1901, only in 1986 did the Australia Act finally sever most ties with Britain by denying Britain the power to make laws for Australia or to exercise any governmental responsibility, and by removing the mechanism of legal appeal to the British Privy Council.

Nonetheless, the Queen of England remains Queen of Australia, represented by the Governor-General since she herself is 20,000 kilometres away. Australia is a member of the British Commonwealth of Nations and there are still some antique clauses squirrelled away in the Australian Constitution: for instance, the Queen of England can still disallow Australian legislation within a year of her Australian Governor-General's having approved it.

For more on this topic, see the section on *The British*, below.

A Jigsaw Nation

Few outsiders realise that Australia was for long no more than a collection of separately autonomous colonies. Nationhood is still a very new thing.

To make matters worse, internal communications and under-standing have been hampered both by the geography of a harsh and huge desert terrain, almost 4000 kilometres from east to west, over 3000 kilometres north to south, and by economic stupidities such as the airline duopoly which made it cheaper to fly abroad than to air-commute internally, until airfare deregulation in late 1990.

The remnants of that early colonial structure, still expressed in the independence of the six state governments, are only now being broken down. For example, only in 1991 was a decision taken to form national bodies which would standardise legal procedures, electrical power, road systems, and the gauge used on railway lines across the country. But whether this will actualy materialse is still in doubt. Inter-state differences have been a great block to economic progress, and to crime-busting too, for many years.

For years until 1991, sausages had differing content regulations in different states, preventing their inter-state sale. Quite often, a single product had to wear different labels and packaging in each different state. There were three definitions of bread; one state demanded that margarine be sold only in cube-shaped packages.

Electricians, plumbers, doctors and lawyers needed licences to work outside their home states. A rail cargo container sent east-west from Sydney to Perth was subject to four changes of locomotive, five safe working systems, six sizes of loading gauge and had to spend 12 hours at sidings for crew changes and inspections.

New moves are now being made to enable the states to raise more of their own revenue by taxation; the Federal Government thus far has raised 80% of all government spending.

HOW AUSSIES SEE SOME OF 'THE OTHERS'

Chapter One dealt with stereotyped images of Australia and Austra-lians. In their attempt to define their own national identity, Australians nurse quite a few stereotypes of their own when it comes to other nationalities, races, creeds and cultures. Understanding these may also help you 'position' yourself better when relating to Australians.

The French

Well, they are not to be trusted and are a reprehensible race by virtue of their nation's espousal of nuclear testing all over the place, and more particularly, on Australia's doorstep, on South Pacific atolls like Mururoa, thus possibly polluting Australian air. Yet, paradoxically, little is said or remembered of British nuclear tests inside Australia itself in the years between 1952 and 1958.

The spontaneous response of an Australian audience to the very mention of the French on a nationwide satire-and-entertainment show, *The Big Gig,* not so long ago, was memorable: 'What are they?' prompted the compere. 'Bastards!' roared the audience spontaneously and with gusto. Similarly, a heading in *The Weekend Australian,* 25–28 September 1993, read simply, 'The Bloody French'.

Some of this Francophobia stems from the famous Australian 'cultural cringe', a condition which nutshells the traditional Australian feeling of inferiority when confronted by European sophistication, history, culture and what-have-you. So when an Australian reviles 'the frogs', he is really only getting his own back for being made to feel small when he fails to cope with a French menu.

Francophobia is also yet another legacy of Australia's British heritage and the historical British hostility to the French.

The British

Better known to Australians as Poms or Pommies (believed to be a reference to their convict past in Australia—Prisoner Of Her Majesty or POHM), the British are also more usually referred to as Pommy Bastards or else, Whingeing Poms. To whinge is to gripe, complain or moan. Aussies believe that the Brits specialise in this art, which they are further alleged to have brought to a high level as shop stewards dominating the Australian trade union movement. The British are therefore to blame for the frequent, economically damaging, strikes in Australia's recent history.

Pommies also do not bath enough, says Australian folklore,

The Round House, 1831, Fremantle, Western Australia. Old prison legacy from Britain. Photo by Siva Choy.

hence the phrase 'As dry as a Pommy's towel (or bathmat)', apparently first coined by the comedian Barry Humphries' Barry McKenzie character.

Traditional ties have weakened considerably since Britain joined the European Economic Community and gradually dropped in her ranking as one of Australia's most important export markets. Tee-shirts emblazoned with such legends as 'Keep Australia Beautiful— Shoot a Pom' and 'Grow Your Own Dope—Plant a Pom' have been sighted.

The paradoxical thing about such attitudes, of course, is that the Queen of England is still Queen of Australia and much white Australian culture derives directly from 'Old Blighty', meaning England. However, this may not be true for much longer, for the Republican movement is intensifying in Australia now—the Australian Labor Party resolved at its national conference in 1991 to seek the status of Republic by 2001.

Republicanism is such a hot issue in Australia that in 1991 debating opponents came to blows on national television. It became a central political issue in the 1992–93 general elections, when Labor pinned its colours to the Republican mast, provoking intense national debate and throwing the traditionalist Liberal party into disarray.

The fact that Labor was re-elected in the face of deep recession is in part indicative of the shift in public opinion towards Republicanism. There is, however, ambivalence about the Australian flag showing the British Union Jack: Labor wants to abandon it but some old hands feel it has been a rallying point of pride, particularly during the two world wars. Recent polls have only 35% of adults favouring any change, and of these 24% say 'not now'. One result of the new climate of opinion is that new Australian citizens no longer have to swear allegiance to the British Queen: they can choose between this old oath or the new one which merely declares their loyalty to Australia.

Since the Queen's accession to the throne in 1953, the Morgan Gallup poll found that the percentage of Australians who want to retain Queen Elizabeth of England as Australia's head of state had fallen from 71% to 56% (1991) and is currently believed to stand between 30% to 40%. The presence of large migrant communities who have no ties to Britain certainly has much to do with this.

Americans

White Australians share many national traits and also historical experiences (such as gold rushes) with the Americans. The two nations are also military allies, together with New Zealand, under the ANZUS security treaty dating from 1952. There are several somewhat mysterious American satellite surveillance and defence installations in Australia's remote heartland. This special relationship however looks a little strained in the context of the US-subsidised wheat sales to China in 1991 which undercut already desperate Australian wheat farmers and exporters.

The two peoples are similarly outgoing, both preferring informality, tending to the brash and loud, and wearing their opinions and

Like American Texans, Aussies like everything Australian to be biggest. Photo by the author.

emotions on their sleeves. They have both conquered a big country (Australia and the mainland USA, excluding Alaska, are almost the same size), including quite a bit of rough terrain.

White Australians too have their cowboys and, in the Aboriginals, their Indians. It is significant perhaps that one of the many delegations of helpers who have visited Australian Aboriginal settlements to advise on coping with social problems like the petrol-sniffing addiction, came from America's Indian reservations, where they share the same problems. The two nations also share the passionate rhetoric of freedom, human rights and democracy.

The two people's languages and their cultures—from drive-in everything and hamburgers to country-and-western music, and of course, television imports—are drawing closer every day. One Australian newspaper columnist recently complained bitterly that somebody had changed the old English word 'torch' to the American 'flashlight' behind his back when he wasn't looking.

In general, there is a feeling of natural affinity. And it must be said, of admiration on the Australian side, despite a regular chorus of complaint against American cultural infiltration. Occasionally, the admiration takes the negative form of 'cultural cringe' (see Chapter One) in relation to American superiority as a world power. For one thing, it is generally agreed, by Australians too, that America saved Australia from a Japanese fate worse than death during World War II.

Everybody, on both sides of the argument, is delighted at the symbolically significant union of quintessential Aussie Paul Hogan ('Crocodile Dundee') with his American leading lady. On the darker side, some Australians to the left of their Labor leaders look askance at Australia's strong defence and security links with the USA, and at the alleged American (and CIA) penetration of the Australian political process.

For a fascinating exposition of this school of thought, among other things, see London-based Australian journalist John Pilger's devastating and controversial book, *A Secret Country*.

Italians and Greeks

Most jokes about the Italians and Greeks are quite good-humoured. After all, an awful lot of Australians can claim Italian or Greek ancestry (almost 2% of Australians even now were actually born in Italy, and about 1% in Greece), and Melbourne in the state of Victoria is accounted the world's second biggest Greek city. The Italian accent is often caricatured, as in the W.A. Salvage advertisements on Perth television, where 'Luigi' genially instructs the viewer on how to 'Sava-Da-Moni'.

It is generally agreed that any houses sporting neo-colonial porticoes, pillars, columns and the like usually prove to belong to, or to have been designed by, nostalgic Italian-Australians—from my own observation, they really do!

New Zealanders

You might imagine that Australians would feel some affinity with the 'Kiwis' of New Zealand, by virtue of being close neighbours, as well as military allies.

Not so. As far as Aussies are concerned, Kiwis are pinching Australian jobs—their passports allow them free entry to and employment in Australia and there are tens of thousands of them in Australia—and are nearly as responsible for the rise in crime as the Vietnamese. Well, almost.

The Australians further resent the Kiwis' often revealed sense of superiority (they do not share the Australians' convict ancestry) and 'English ways'. There is really little love lost between them.

The Tasmanians

Now, this is an awkward one. Tasmanians (often jocularly referred to as Taswegians) are Australians. But you wouldn't think so from the way most mainlander Australians talk about them.

Tasmania (affectionately known as Tassie, pronounced 'Tazzie') is Australia's smallest state and an island, 240 kilometres off the southeastern corner of the mainland, with a population of less than half a million spread over more than 67,000 square kilometres.

Tasmanians are a standing joke in mainland Australia. The basic premise of every Tasmanian joke is that Tasmanians are hillbillies and country bumpkins (including lonely farmers habituated to questionable sexual practices) afflicted with the mental and physical consequences of extensive inbreeding: hence the many jokes referring to them as having 'two heads', 'pointy-heads' and the like.

Racists? Not Really

I mention all the above as a prelude to answering the question, 'Are Australians racist?'

The answer really is No, they are equally rude about absolutely everybody, of whatever colour or creed. This is partly because, despite the difficulties encountered in defining the 'typical Australian', they have a very real sense of their own identity, and a concomitant sense of isolation, both cultural and geographical, from 'the others'. The Australian racist, when he does surface, in any case may well prove to be something else as well—an Australian of British, Dutch or South African origin, for example.

There is some survey evidence that young, mostly teenage, Australians are racist to some degree. I myself have encountered Australian teenagers firmly declaring that all South Asians 'smell'. But this conforms with a pattern of youth conservatism now sweeping the world and cannot be said to be exclusively Australian.

The perceived 'Aboriginal problem' with which white Australia is grappling—of which more later—tends to add further fuel to the fires of racism, partly through the nation's collective guilt over the terrible wrongs done to Aboriginal Australians in the past, partly because the gap between white society and aboriginal society is highly visible. There is much truth in the view that Australia will never be whole as a nation until there is full reconciliation between white and black Australians.

But finally, we all have to ask ourselves: which nation is truly without racism? Everyone should examine their own glass house carefully before throwing careless stones. The important thing is, are racist opinions sanctioned or encouraged at the top? And are real efforts being made to discourage them on the ground? In Australia, there is no official support for racism; quite the contrary, in fact.

Poor Australia is in fact hoist by her own petard: her free and open climate for debate. In Australia, racism is publicly discussed (this is not true of all other countries) which makes the topic more visible, and Australia more vulnerable to outsider-critics. I shall discuss this topic again, in the next chapter and in the chapter on Aboriginal Australia.

Asians

Before we talk about Australian attitudes to Asians, let us first translate the word 'Asian' into Australian: it means, almost exclusively, Chinese and Vietnamese, and perhaps sometimes Japanese too. It does not usually refer to Indians, for example. In other words, it refers to those of Mongoloid stock. Among racists, it is a euphemism for 'slant-eyes'. This is quite different of course from the meaning the word 'Asian' has acquired in, say, London or Birmingham, UK, where it is used to refer to South Asians, i.e. those originating from India, Pakistan or Sri Lanka.

Australians are only now recovering from their White Australia era. And they are recovering very quickly, too. Nowadays you can barely open a newspaper or magazine without seeing some discussion of the new Multicultural Australia.

Australia is striving very hard to make this dream a reality. Children are learning Chinese, Japanese, Malay and Indonesian at school these days; such studies are already compulsory in the schools of some states, although 1989 figures still showed only 3% of Australian secondary students studying Asian languages. The government expects to have Asian studies courses in all Australian schools by 1995.

There are also countless new research and study centres specialising in strengthening Australia's links with Asia: for example, the Australian-Indonesian Institute established in 1989 to promote people-to-people contact, and the federally funded Asia Research Centre attached to Murdoch University in Western Australia, established in 1991.

The country deserves some sympathy and understanding for making the effort in the first place. And multiculturalism should not be one-sided. While Australians 'give it a go' and try to understand myriad alien cultures, surely newly arrived guests should reciprocate?

The White Australia Policy

The White Australia policy dated back to the 1901 Restrictive Immigration Act which kept out non-European immigrants, following an influx of cheap Chinese labour to the Australian goldfields after the 1840s.

Among other things, the policy produced silly situations like the case of twin brothers with mixed parenthood, one looking Indian and the other European. No prizes for guessing which one got in and which one didn't. And many a southern European was rejected for immigration in those days, on the grounds of being a touch too swarthy.

The attitudes of those times spawned a rash of consumer products like Golden Fleece Soap, which said it would 'Keep Australia White'. This policy was not abandoned till 1973. Up to that date, Australians were taught to be afraid of the 'Yellow Peril' from the north, be it Japanese or Indonesian. It takes time to shake off such grim instruction.

Yet, curiously, I must mention here that a Chinese-Australian and Sri-Lankan-Australian friend of mine, both of whom arrived in Western Australia long before 1973, have told me that they were well treated at that time, 'like guests, like a special novelty'. Even today, I can report that a Chinese friend was hosted to a welcome tea-party by his new Aussie neighbours and another Chinese lady regularly exchanges cooked dishes from her kitchen for handyman fixing about her house by her Australian neighbour.

That said, quite a few Australians do believe that the Vietnamese have brought an increase in crime (proportionately, in fact, they generate less than their share of national crime), that other Asians have brought exotic diseases like tuberculosis and hepatitis B, and that migrant Asians are taking Australians' jobs. You will find similar misconceptions about immigrants in almost every country experiencing a sudden influx of them.

Cultural Burps and Misunderstandings

Considering the country's long isolation from Asia under the White Australia policy and considering the rapid social change, if not turmoil, that large-scale Asian immigration has brought about over the past decade or so, it's surprising there is not more overt racism in Australia.

However, let us now 'sensitise' ourselves by looking at some of the things that can trigger Australian hostility.

Like the Chinese man I saw spit upon the marbled pavements of the luxurious Burswood Casino Hotel in Perth, Western Australia.

Like the Vietnamese I saw haggling over a few cents at a simple Australian neighbourhood second-hand sales fair, where nothing was priced much more than A$5. How to explain in a few seconds to the offended Australian vendors the long tradition of bargaining in Southeast Asia? How to explain to the Vietnamese that there was an unspoken gentleman's agreement that such friendly markets were fixed-price?

Like the Chinese students I saw yelling and shouting in their native Mandarin at an Australian university bus-stop, without any regard for how uncomfortable it made the Australian commuters around them feel: 'Are we in Australia, or what?'

Like the Singapore tourists at Perth hotel buffets who piled their plates high with food they couldn't finish, simply to get their money's worth, leaving behind mountains of wasted food.

Or the Asian shoppers who transferred their market customs to their local Australian supermarket, poking their fingers into fruit and vegetables, and test-eating some of them, 'not done' in Australia. The Japanese tourist who poured tomato ketchup over his breakfast cereal didn't go down too well either.

The Mystery of the Vanishing Abalone

Then there is the abalone problem off Western Australian coasts. For decades or more, ordinary Australians have enjoyed their annual abalone harvest, sticking firmly to the rules, or so they claim: take no more than 20 pieces per person per day and leave the small ones alone, to generate future stocks.

But in 1991, the Western Australian state government had to cancel that year's fishing season outright. There was no abalone left and it looked likely there might not be much more in future either. Who dunnit? 'The Vietnamese,' said some Aussies. 'The Chinese,' said others. 'All Asians,' said yet others. 'Not us,' chorused the Asians. It was the big boys, the Australians with the commercial interests.

Obviously, the Western Australian Fisheries Minister at that time, Gordon Hill, thought somebody not English-speaking had done it: among the measures he announced when cancelling the season was a multilingual education programme for fishermen.

And columnist Mike Roennfeldt, writing in *The West Australian* newspaper said: 'Everyone, including the media, has been so terrified of being labelled racists that the obvious truth has been ignored. It seems to me that tippy-toeing around the fact that the whole abalone problem lies directly at the feet of Australians of Asian descent is actually being more racist than facing squarely up to the truth.'

Whatever the rights and wrongs of this case, it is a good example of why some Australians may have reservations about Asians.

A very similar thorn in Australian flesh is the Indonesian 'poaching' of Australia's valuable trochus shell. Between 1989 and 1991, Australian patrol boats arrested 150 Indonesian vessels, mostly from Sulawesi, for fishing inside Australian waters, in a multi-million dollar campaign to stop illegal fishing.

From the Indonesian fishermen's point of view, fishing off Australia, for fish and shellfish, for trochus and for sea-slug (known as *trepang*), is a centuries-old traditional right, which in many cases they had negotiated amicably with the indigenous Aboriginals. Besides, they are poor and desperate enough to just keep on coming.

To top all this off, Australians generally feel that Asian societies are reprehensible for their lack of social and political freedom, in short, for not being like Australia.

The rows with Malaysia over first, the 1986 hanging in Malaysia of two Australians, Kevin Barlow and Brian Chambers, for carrying drugs (Australia does not have the death penalty for any crime), and then the ABC TV screening in 1990–91 of a soap opera titled *Embassy* set in a fictional Southeast Asian Muslim country called Ragaan, which just happened to be located between the borders of Thailand and Malaysia, are cases in point.

The series *was* insulting to Malaysia. But the Australian government does not control the country's media, a simple fact which many Asians find very difficult to understand in the context of their own 'guided' media.

The Challenge of the Crescent Moon

Islam is indeed a topic calculated to raise the hairs on the back of many an Australian neck. This reaction stems from a blend of ignorance and blind fear. Australians are not alone in this.

People in Middle Eastern dress, especially women in veils, are too visibly different on Australian streets. Iraqi president Saddam Hussein's Gulf War in 1990–91 hardly helped. It will take great patience and tolerance on both sides if this barrier is to be breached.

It certainly was alarming to hear white Australian residents on the eastern side of Australia reacting to the prospect of a mosque being erected in their neighbourhood. They howled their opposition. Their reason: property values would slump (unfortunately, possible), and 'the kiddies wouldn't be safe to walk home,' as one woman-in-the-street put it to the TV cameras, a revelation of shocking prejudice.

But on the more positive side, when I tuned in to an ABC radio programme on the subject of Iraq, during the Gulf War, while fully expecting to hear more of the same, I was pleasantly surprised. (The topic was whether or not Iraqis and the Arabs in Australia—particularly Australians with Arab ancestry—should be allowed to demonstrate against Australia's anti-Iraq stand, as they had already done.)

Many of those who called into the radio station were themselves migrants to Australia way back, just after World War II—from Britain, from Germany, from Eastern Europe. Of 15 callers, seven said, No, Arabs in Australia should not be allowed to demonstrate against Australian government policy, while a majority of eight said, Yes, absolutely, they must have the same democratic right to protest as other Australians, but they must not be allowed to burn the Australian flag, or commit acts of violence.

Not that racism failed to rear its ugly head. That could not be, in a full-blooded democracy like Australia's, where even the far right must be allowed to have its say. Just for the record, there was one caller who declared flatly: 'No I reckon we should not have Arabs in this country. I reckon they are all mad.'

But try telling all this to my Singaporean-Malay and Muslim friend, who is married to an Australian girl of Roman Catholic Italian parentage, Cindy, and lives in Perth. Cindy is now a good Muslim—the couple have found a mosque in Perth to attend every Friday—and she produces fine Malaysian food every year for the Muslim feast of Ramadan, at the end of the fasting month, clad in traditional Malay dress.

Does she ever get teased or harassed about her new religion? 'No, no—not at all,' she smiles gently. End of conversation.

The Japanese

Then there is the Australian unease about the Japanese, who admittedly own huge chunks of their country, most notably in Queensland, where they hold about 93% of all foreign-owned hotel rooms, for example.

This unease is deepened by actual or culturally inherited memories of the Pacific War during World War II, during which Australian soldiers, like many others, suffered bitterly at the hands of the Japanese. Reactions to the recent death of the wartime Emperor Hirohito of Japan were not pleasant: there was unmistakable jubilation in the air at times. But such sentiment is by no means exclusively Australian.

I have already remarked elsewhere that it is a serious impediment to happiness in Australia not to be able to speak English. The Japanese often suffer from this inability. Columnist Ruth Ostrow, writing in *The Weekend Australian*, reported with outrage how a Japanese tourist was made fun of in a Gold Coast hotel bar. He kept ordering Scotch without ice. Each time, it came back with ice. 'No locks, no locks!' he kept yelling. The waitress and staff erupted into giggles every time.

The Asian Future

But Australia knows she must come to terms with Asia, as a matter of economic survival if nothing else.

The country's first ambassador to China, Stephen Fitzgerald, himself a fluent Mandarin speaker, noted recently that of the 35 finalist companies entered in the 1987 Australian Export Awards contest, 24 employed people who were fluent in one or more languages such as Japanese, Chinese, Arabic or French.

On the other hand, two-thirds of the companies recently surveyed by the Australian Department of Employment, Education and Training were exporting 85% of their sales to English-speaking countries. With the huge single markets of Europe and America-Canada-Mexico looming large on the world stage and likely to turn in on themselves, this hardly seems wise.

And, by 1990, International Monetary Fund figures already showed per capita GNP in countries like Singapore (US$9,620) and Hong Kong (US$8,418) to be edging close to Australia's US$12,590, while Japan had already left Australia behind, with its per capita

GNP of US$19,553. There has been much talk in Australia of late about the 'middle-classing' of Asia: a belated recognition of the buying power in Asia's markets.

Besides, within the next 40 years, something like 20% of Australia's population is likely to be of Asian origin. Australia will not only be a part of Asia, as it must be on the basis of geography alone, but Asia will already be a part of Australia.

NATION

National Flag The Australian Blue Ensign (for merchant ships, the Australian Red Ensign). This blue flag has a British Union Jack in the upper left corner, closest to the flagpole, with the seven-pointed Commonwealth star below it; to the right are the five stars of the Southern Cross constellation, identified as 'Crux Australis' as early as 1679, seen only in southern skies such as Australia's. Now that talk of a Republic is active, there is a lobby for a completely new 'Ausflag', possibly using the national colours of green and gold. But the debate is by no means over yet.

National Animal Emblem Kangaroo.

National Flower Emblem The Golden Wattle. Australia boasts about 900 species of this desert-adapted tree or shrub, which belongs to the Mimosa family within the Acacia genus.

National Colours Green and gold.

National Coat of Arms Granted in 1912 by King George V of England, the shield is supported by a kangaroo and an emu amid branches of wattle.

National Anthem Up to 1974, the British national anthem, *God Save The Queen*, was also Australia's, but in 1974 a national poll replaced it with the 19th century song *Advance Australia Fair*. *God Save The Queen* is now only played when the Queen herself or her representative, the Governor-General, is present.

— *Chapter Four* —

BEING A MIGRANT

'The lazy country will be the lovely country, the white society will be the honey-coloured society, and the ugly duckling will become a honey-coloured swan.'
—Dr Stephen Fitzgerald, Australia's first ambassador to China,
as head of the University of New South Wales Asia Centre,
in *The West Australian*, November 24, 1990.

This chapter is not a detailed guide to the labyrinth of getting permission to migrate to Australia. It just gives a snapshot of what it is like to be a migrant, and what migration has meant to Australia.

Even if I wanted to give you a detailed 'how to do it' guide, I doubt I could. For a start, the rules of the immigration game change fairly often—signposts to change usually are imminent federal elections and economic upheaval. The current recession has put the Labor government under further pressure to restrict immigration on the grounds that it is useless to import more people if you cannot give them jobs. There does seem to be some sense in this argument, if you view it objectively. As a result of economic recession, making Australia less attractive to migrants, and lowering government quotas, immigration levels are now down to about 80,000 a year.

Some analysts sincerely feel that mass immigration, peaking at 172,000 newcomers in 1988, the year when recommendations that the level be fixed at 140,000 per year in future were accepted by the government, takes out of the economy more than it contributes.

There is also the fear of potential social tension, hitherto largely and happily avoided.

The Shifting Sands of Immigration Policy
As an example of the rapid shifts in policy, when I was applying to migrate, in the mid-1980s, it was possible to become a Business Migrant and virtually buy your way into Australia providing you could prove you had A$500,000 capital to invest, a business to run, and enough funds to keep yourself and your family for a set period of time. (I hasten to add that this did not apply to me.) Some 9000 business migrants were admitted to Australia on this basis between 1983 and 1991, bringing in A$1.5 billion. It was also possible to bring in your aged parents once you yourself had settled in Australia for a while, on the grounds of 'family reunion'.

Another category of accepted migrant at that time was the foreign man or woman who intended marriage with an Australian, or even

Sydney's old Queen Victoria Building was restored as a shopping arcade by Asian investment. Photo by Siva Choy.

those who had a *de facto* rather than a *de jure* relationship with an Australian—in other words, whether they were going to get married or not.

By 1991, all three of these programmes had disappeared, largely because of migrants' abuse of the system. The Business Migrant programme was ditched because cunning would-be migrants, many of them Asian, were simply recycling lumps of money from one applicant to the next, and then failing to run a business in Australia. Now business skills are checked carefully and the business migrant is required to invest in government bonds and his business monitored.

At the time of writing, the rule on importing aged parents is that the parent in question must already have half or more of all their children settled in Australia, otherwise, sorry, the door is closed.

As for the migration-for-marriage scheme, naturally that led to so many marriage-of-convenience scams, with Australian girls often being paid handsomely to go through mock marriages with foreign-

Alec Fong Lim, late Mayor of Darwin, a symbol of what the migrant can achieve in Australia.

ers, that it had to be curbed. The sad result is that genuine lovers now have to go through a lot more hoops to prove that their marriage to an Australian is bona fide before they can get residence in Australia.

The Grey Face of Australian Bureaucracy

Sometimes the rules are uncomfortably vague. For example, there has been a great deal of confusion over how long you have to stay in Australia to confirm your permanent residence as a migrant. As a migrant myself, I have never received any official written or verbal instruction on this matter. Here again, you see a fine example of how grey areas develop in Australian policy, purely because Australians have a democratic horror of the tyranny of rigid law: this leaves everyone in the dark.

However, it also means there is flexibility—a smile and a nod could well win the day, whereas in many other countries, rules are rules, and there's no way round them.

It is true, at the time of writing, that if you want to apply for Australian citizenship, you must spend 24 months in Australia, not necessarily consecutively, within your first three-year migrant's visa, or within your first five years in Australia—which is in fact a very generous provision. If you want simple renewal of your three-year migrant residence visa for another 12 months you will need to show 12 months' (non-consecutive) residence in Australia within the first three years. Spouses of Australian citizens will more easily get a five-year renewal.

But it's anyone's guess half the time, and really, the horse's mouth has to be your local Australian High Commission or Embassy. Note that policy changes can be dramatic at times of elections (compulsorily every three years), especially if there is a change of ruling party.

Familiarisation Techniques

Would-be migrants would be well advised to read the Australian press for at least a year before they make their move. I myself subscribed to *The Weekend Australian* for a year before I migrated, and picked up the odd copy of my local *The West Australian* daily whenever I could find one. *The Age* of Melbourne and the *Australian Financial Review,* besides the weekly *The Bulletin,* are also good backgrounders.

It's a good idea too to have visited Australia before you decide to migrate there. This may sound like unnecessary advice, but not if my husband is anything to go by: a Singaporean-Indian, he was determined to migrate there without ever having set foot in the country.

Because he is black, I was just a wee bit nervous and insisted he travel across the country both with and without me first. This he did—and came back singing its praises even more loudly. So we filled in the forms, got all our official documents legally certified in multiplicate (a tedious and expensive business) and settled down to something like an 18-month wait before we got the good news.

The Questions Some Migrants Ask

Unquestionably the funniest experience we had in the migration process was the group counselling session at the Australian High Commission in Singapore. Once upon a time, it had been possible to offer individual counselling interviews to accepted migrants, but as numbers rose, this was abandoned in favour of group meetings.

The questions we heard asked by the predominantly Asian-Singaporean migrants at our session boggled the imagination. I take my hat off to the extremely patient immigration officer who had to handle them. She did so in typically Australian dry, wry style.

The session kicked off with 'When I come to Australia, can I bring my servant with me?' No, was the answer, ours is a do-it-yourself society. A shy couple was worried: considering the strict quarantine laws, could they bring into Australia the kangaroo skin which they had bought in Australia on a holiday? 'No worries' was the not unexpected answer to that one.

A strapping young man with no apparent health problems was extremely interested in how soon after landing he could qualify for Medicare (the subsidised medical service), the dole (social welfare payments for the unemployed) and a state pension. One could somehow guess what direction he was going in and I am sure the beleaguered immigration officer privately labelled him a potential bludger on the spot (see the Glossary in Chapter Two).

Agitated beyond belief was a Chinese man who asked whether or not he could regularly import Chinese dried mushrooms to Australia after setting up home there. Life, it seemed, would be meaningless without them. Food-import controls were strict, said the officer, and anyway, Australia grew perfectly good mushrooms of her own. No, no, insisted the Chinese, I mean our black mushrooms, our *Chinese* ones, you know? The implication seemed to be that no Australian mushroom could ever be a match for a Chinese one.

Of course, yours truly, being English, was concerned only whether or not she could import her pet dog. The answer to that one is, only if you want to go through a very long, expensive and potentially traumatic quarantine clearance process. For example, if I had wanted to take my dog from Singapore to Australia, it would have had to be cleared first for six months at an approved centre outside of Asia, like London or Hawaii, after which it would undergo three more months of quarantine in Australia itself. I could not countenance either the expense of the implied airfares and kennelling charges or the emotional trauma to the dog. She stayed put in Singapore.

You Can Take It With You

What *can* you take into Australia when you go? Probably everything you own, although as much as possible should be over 12 months old, and you should have the documentation to prove this.

When my husband and I first landed, we had a typed checklist of the property we were carrying with us (including a large fax machine I had refused to ship, because I needed it immediately for work), complete with every item's value, age and serial number. This was much appreciated by Customs, and speeded clearance considerably.

The rest of the documentation should be handled by your freight-forwarding agent, who will let you know whether or not you are required to be present for a meeting with Customs when your cargo arrives. In our case, we were not.

Some items can be a particular problem: for example wooden objects or cane/bamboo/rattan may be treated as a hazard to Australian agriculture because of the bugs they may hide, and this will mean careful fumigation at the very least. Once again, with such problems, you should check carefully on the latest rules with your nearest Australian government representative office.

But remember, once you have taken up residence in Australia, you will be travelling as an Australian; when you re-enter Australia, your allowance for purchases (such as radios from Singapore and the like) will be restricted to a value of A\$400 per head. Anything above that must be declared, with a supporting document proving its sale value.

If you are travelling regularly in and out of Australia with an expensive item of equipment—a lap-top computer, say—we have found it useful to ask Customs to note down the serial number on a Customs form before leaving Australia, so that you can later prove you did not buy it on your trip abroad and are therefore not liable for duty. Customs will often tell you there is no need to worry when you first approach them with this one, but we suggest you insist in case the next Customs officer is less understanding.

In general, when returning to Australia, we have found that honest declaration when in doubt really pays. On the few occasions when we have had to pay duty, we have always found it very reasonable, being usually around 20% of the sale value, above your A$400 allowance.

Toughing It Out

But don't get too smart by arranging for under-invoicing at a fantastic bargain-basement price; Australian Customs officers know very well what are the likely selling prices for most items, whether you are coming from Singapore or from London. Like Customs officers everywhere, they react pretty brutally if they discover you have been trying to take them for a ride.

Be careful too with illicitly-copied computer software: Australia strictly enforces copyright protection laws.

Never, ever try to sneak in food or plant material (that includes cut roses and orchids, Mum's home-made jam and Auntie's fantastic curry powder) without declaring it. It's a very serious offence. You may get it approved if you declare it; or like my friend with the tupperware of unwrapped smelly cheese he didn't want to leave behind in his fridge at home, you might not.

Everyone has had at least one horror story with Australian Immigration/Customs officials. They can be toughies, although they come on initially with brighter smiles and more friendly chat than any of their counterparts worldwide. At least, the men do. So relax. But take my tip: never get in the queue for a woman immigration or

Customs officer's desk. I would like to be more sisterly, but for some reason, they are much nastier than the men.

I shall not easily forget one such unsmiling lady at Perth airport who had our entire luggage searched, apparently for drugs, just because we had travelled in and out of Malaysia once too often for her liking. Nor how she thrust her hands triumphantly into the tatty, torn silk lining of my suitcase—at last, a false bottom—flipped suspiciously through the pages of my notebooks, and even had my Indonesian wooden puppets' heads X-rayed for secret compartments.

By comparison, the men are more laid-back, but therefore also fallible. Although emotionally scarred, we survived one of our migrant residence visas being accidentally cancelled at the airport (inspect your passport carefully to see what has been done before you leave the airport)—a frightening discovery made only just before our next flight.

On balance, though, a cool temper combined with a modest and pleasant demeanour will see you through. No showing off, please. One well-heeled Chinese visitor learned his lesson. Asked what he had come to Australia for, he facetiously replied, 'To spend money.' This was not a sensitive remark in the context of the Australian recession and the average Customs officer's salary. Needless to say, they took him apart.

What Use Are Migrants?

Why then, does Australia want migrants? Well, some segments of Australian society in fact do not want them at all. Others would prefer them to come from white Europe. But all major political parties currently accept migration as necessary. All are agreed that willy-nilly, Australia must have more people than its current 17.7 million, to gain economic strength, to build a bigger internal market. (There is a contrary minority view, however, which holds that immigration may well exceed the unique, desert-bound Australian ecology's natural 'carrying capacity' for a limited number of humans.)

Disagreements tend to focus on how many should be admitted, and what type—European or Asian, skilled or unskilled, English-speaking or not, and so on. In the old days, it was believed that the only way to resist the 'Yellow Peril' from the north was to breed and multiply—'Populate or Perish', the slogan went. Nowadays, the official credo is that, to integrate with the booming economies of Asia, Australia needs Asian immigration.

Immigration doesn't just make money by stimulating the economy; it makes money *per se*. Migrants brought A$4.3 billion into Australia in 1989 alone, making immigration the nation's third biggest earner after tourism and wool at the time.

The same things are said about unwanted immigrants all over the world, no matter which cultures are involved: they contribute to social disorder, they cause rises in crime, they import new diseases, they pinch local jobs ... In Australia, they said it about the Greeks and Italians, even the British, when they first arrived; they say it now about the Vietnamese, Chinese and Japanese—and some of the people saying it today are in fact Italian-Australians, British-Australians and the like, former migrants themselves.

Each generation of immigrants must undergo its own baptism of fire, emerging tempered from the crucible.

A Migrant Nation

Much is said nowadays about Asian migration to Australia. It is sometimes forgotten that between mid-1947 and the end of 1951, Australia took in 170,000 of post-World War II Europe's 12 million displaced people. There is a fascinating account of this programme, written both from the point of view of Immigration officers and migrants in a study titled *Angels and Arrogant Gods,* from the Australian Commonwealth Government Publishing Service.

At first it was 'whites only, please'. Migrant Britons were offered financially-assisted passage to Australia from 1946 to 1982, when the practice was discontinued. Many an Asian and other migrant today arrives by plane with a substantial bank balance (having sold a house back home), a container-load of possessions and university qualifications to boot.

It is humbling to reflect on the fact that those early European migrants often arrived in Australia only after a harrowing journey aboard an overcrowded ship, without a penny in their pockets and committed to a compulsory work contract (usually hard manual labour) with the Australian government in some remote corner of the country, where they were housed in makeshift huts at best.

You had to stay two years before the government would even give you your passport back. But then, where you had come from, you didn't even have food …

Such were the original New Australians. There was no talk about 'multiculturalism' in those days. You were supposed to become Australian, as quickly and as convincingly as possible.

It was not until Gough Whitlam's Labor Party came to power in 1972 that the racist immigration policy was finally laid to rest. In 1976, the first Senior Immigration Officer was appointed to an Asian posting. These changes came just in time to accommodate the Vietnamese boat-people refugees of the 1970s. By 1986, Australia had taken in more than 100,000 Indochinese refugees. The total number of refugees from all sources taken into Australia between 1945 and 1985, however, was a massive 430,000.

Before mass migration programmes began, back in 1947, fewer than one in 10 Australians had been born outside the country. The population then was about seven million. Today, about a quarter of Australians are either first or second-generation immigrants and more than two-thirds are of mixed ethnic origin. Australia is a country of 130 nations. Some Sydney suburbs are 42% of non-English speaking origin. By 2021, one-quarter of Australians will be foreign-born; the total population then should be about 25 million if present migration patterns continue. By the year 2010, say some studies, the Chinese-origin population of Australia alone could exceed one million.

Multiculturalism—Handle With Care

Beyond simple migration, the Labor government has further es-
poused multiculturalism within Australia and has put its money
where its mouth is.

Multiculturalism is reckoned to cost the Federal and State Governments about A\$514 million a year, or about A\$30 for each
Australian, revealed *The Australian* newspaper in its own 1991
investigation. These costs are incurred in a range of activities, from
the Special Broadcasting Service (SBS) catering to minority culture,
to ethnic language booklets on everything under the sun and English-
as-a-second-language programmes.

This policy worries even some proponents of Asian migration, let
alone conservatives concerned with preserving Australia's British
heritage. They worry about 'ghetto-ism'.

The recent upheavals in Eastern Europe amply demonstrated the
problem, as did the Gulf War of 1990–91: émigré communities of
Serbs and Croats in Australia avoided, or attacked, one another in
tandem with the factions developing in what was Yugoslavia, while
Romanian-Australians denounced the Ceausescu 'moles' in their
midst after the Romanian revolutionaries had despatched their former
dictator. I even know of a Eurasian group which has fractured along
lines demarcated by whether one is of Dutch/English or Portuguese
origin.

Many migrants and refugees have, perhaps understandably, im-
ported their domestic political and social problems into Australia.
These nations within a nation have made many uneasy.

This is an ongoing debate, as it is in some other countries too, such
as Britain: should migrants be forced or persuaded into cultural
integration? For instance, can Muslims be obliged to submit to
Australian customs and laws?

America demonstrates that there can be solutions. I myself am
confident that Australia too will cope, eventually. 'She'll be right.'

Rubbing Shoulders with the World

As a migrant yourself, you may well find multiculturalism exciting. For the first time, you will find yourself side by side with exotic cultures you never dreamed of encountering before.

How, for instance, could my Sri Lankan engineer friend ever have guessed he would end up marrying a Colombian girl in Australia? Listening to the interplay of this family's three different accents when conversing together in English at their Australian dinner-table is something of a treat: his voice still heavily Indian-inflected, hers distinctly Spanish, and their little girl's, why Australian, of course.

You may have to be more careful than you were before. I have already mentioned how problematic 'Irish jokes' may be in the wrong company. There are other potential social gaffes to avoid: you may find it next to impossible to mix your Serb and Croat friends from Yugoslavia, for example, and it would be most ill-advised to invite an Armenian and a Turk, or a Tamil and a Sinhalese, together for tea.

Yet multiculturalism is a furnace in which hitherto unheard-of new alliances may be forged: I think, for instance, of the Portugal Day hosted by the Portuguese Consul in Perth, which saw peoples of all the former Portuguese colonies come together in song, dance and festivity: from Indonesian Timor, from African Mozambique, from Latin American Brazil, from Goa in India, from Malacca in Malaysia and from Macau off China. And yet they were all Australians too.

Indeed, one's definition of an 'Australian' blurs somewhat when confronted with pedigrees like those of my friends. Former residents of Singapore, they now live in Perth. My girlfriend's mother was born in Shanghai and looks Chinese, but doesn't speak the language. (Her parents were Czech-Japanese on one side, Irish-Chinese on the other.) My girlfriend's father, on the other hand, was a Latvian who had fled his Baltic home-state during the Russian Revolution of 1917, to Shanghai via Siberia; in Shanghai, he had been adopted by a benevolent Iraqi-Jewish opium trader.

This couple got out of China in 1954, using the wife's part-Czech descent as a pretext for exit. And so to Singapore, where my ostensibly Singaporean, now Australian, girlfriend was born to them.

My girlfriend's husband is a mixed Irish-Eurasian from Singapore. Should anyone be surprised that their little girl has turned out fair and freckled of skin, with stunning red hair? I challenge anyone to top this family on the multiculturalism scoreboard.

Multiculturalism and the promotion of ethnic politics has led to ethnic lobbying. Former Malaysian-Chinese Dr Eric Tan, a prominent surgeon and community leader in Perth, has a shrewd idea of future directions. Himself an 'Asian-Australian' for 30 years now, he told me, 'You can expect a trend towards the Chinese community entering Australian politics Australia-wide.'

It seems a Chinese-Australian Prime Minister of Australia may well be on the cards. There is already one Bill O'Chee of Queensland, at 24 the youngest person ever elected to the Australian Senate (for the National Party, straight from the rural heartlands), in 1990, whose grandfather was China-born but Irish-ised his name to 'O'Chee' to fob off Australian racism. Bill's mother is Irish, his father Chinese.

Integration Without Tears

You, as a migrant, should at least be sensitive to Australian concerns about multiculturalism. It is natural, and also helpful in the initial stages of migration, to turn to support organisations comprising your former compatriots. In every Australian city, you will find the right club for yourself: Greek, Italian, Polish, Serb, Croat, Tamil, Malayalee, Sri Lankan, Timorese, Eurasian, Singaporean or what-have-you.

But you would do well to make an effort to meet Australians by joining some of their activities too—from your street Neighbourhood Watch (crime-watch) committee, to the local church, the local heritage/history society, or a nature-walking group. Trouble is, you find that many of the 'Australians' around you prove to be migrants too. But even this discovery serves to make you feel more at home, less of an oddity.

Remember that Australia is remarkable for the ease with which you can strike up a conversation with a stranger. Don't be shy, speak up if you want to make friends, whether on the bus or when picking up the children from school along with other parents. This dictum applies especially to naturally conservative Asians.

Remember too that elaborate structures are already in existence to help migrants: consult your local phone directory for contact with bodies like the Ethnic Communities Council or the Multicultural and Ethnic Affairs Commission. Ask them for advice, and the contacts for other migrant assistance centres.

As for general information, if you look up your phone directory listing for Recorded Information Services, or letter 'D' for 'Dial-It', you will be astounded at the range of things you can find out over the phone. Similarly, Australia excels in the prolific production of first-class information leaflets and brochures. A browsing session at your local library, Council and other local government offices, as well as hospitals, and medical and migrant resource centres, will harvest a sheaf of such literature.

Take an active interest in Australian politics and social issues by reading the local press; sample typical Australian activities, such as the local footy (Australian rules football) or cricket matches. Watch television and listen to the radio; make a point of seeing the latest Australian movies and plays, art exhibitions and so on. This will help you converse with Australians on their own ground. Talk about your homeland's politics only with your own kind; don't bore an Australian with them, unless you are sure he finds them riveting.

If, by any chance, your English is less than perfect, work on it. The language is crucial to your integration.

Mum's the Word about Home

In the same box comes the problem of the 'Back home, we do it this way …' syndrome. Avoid at all costs making public comparisons, particularly invidious ones, between your motherland and your newly adopted home, Australia. This goes down very badly with Australians. Put yourself in their place and this becomes very easy to understand. Listen, Look and Learn—But Keep Quiet.

The Migrant Blues

No matter how gungho you have been initially about making a new life in Australia, there will come those moments when you feel depressed, alienated … You wonder if you have made a mistake. This applies to all—and I include those of Anglo-Saxon background, who may be all the more shocked to discover how 'foreign' Australia can be. How much more, non-European migrants.

In many ways, the respectable, older middle-class migrant may suffer more, and more silently, from culture shock than a refugee. For refugees, there are all sorts of support and aid groups. For simple migrants—once you land, you're on your own, mate. The older you are, the harder it is. You will find that your young children, in contrast, take to it like a duck to water.

You must accept that it usually takes something like two or three years before you feel comfortable, begin to 'fit'. Whatever you do, don't give up before you have given it a go for a couple of years. Believe that it will get better. Statistics show that migrants usually quit within the first three years, but rarely later than that.

It's the little things that get you down.

For those used to lively, noisy city streets and housing estates at night, it can be the lack of people, the silence of the dimly lit streets of suburbia. Residential areas resemble menacing black holes at night: Australians seem to live mostly at the back of the house, turning off all the lights at the front as an economy measure, leaving a faceless and unwelcoming streetscape.

A Singaporean Malay friend in Perth recently bought a plot of land and decided to build his own house on it. When I looked at his plans, I exclaimed, 'But why have you chosen to live so close to a highway?'

'It's the silence,' said he. 'I just can't stand it. I just have to have more noise, else I get lonely.'Some call it peaceful, others lonely.

No more food-stalls or cafés in the street, unlike Singapore, Kuala Lumpur, Athens or Paris. Faced with steep restaurant prices and early closing times, you do more home entertaining than ever before. Not a soul on the streets; and it's not all that safe to walk the streets alone at night, either. And in the winter, well, you wouldn't want to.

Beaten, you retreat behind the four walls of your home like the rest of Australia. Having read the over-active local press for the latest, often horrific, crime stories, you fearfully lock up the house and barricade your bedroom door with chairs for good measure.

Unfortunately, in the setting of Australia's high unemployment rate of around 10%, or more, fear of crime is justified. It was only yesterday that Perth-dwellers still left their doors and windows open all the time, and never locked their cars, but alas, no more. I myself was greeted by a friendly brick through my window before I even moved into my new house. Just a minor burglary attempt, but still ...

I got a burglar alarm and paid a monthly fee to connect it to a monitoring station that would call the police if it went off. I would recommend a dog too if you have the time to maintain one, as well as metal grille-reinforcements to windows and doors.

Transportation

If you have never driven before, which was the case with me, thanks to tiny Singapore's excellent public transportation and punitive car costs, those four walls of home quickly become a cosy cage.

The transportation situation is the reverse in huge Australia. One of the keys to happiness in Australia is having a driving licence: don't leave without it. (If you hold one already, you'll probably only need to pass a simple oral test within a few months of arrival in Australia in order to convert it to an Australian licence—but check this with your local police station.)

Mum, your favourite nanny, is no longer just around the corner; your best friend no longer just a phone call away.

More Bummers

For those accustomed to 24-hour shopping—as many Asians are—it takes some getting used to that one must get to the shops by 5.30 p.m. on a weekday. Or to remember that Thursday is late shopping night (in Perth, anyway). Forget Sundays (except for that nice Thai lady's delicatessen shop, and the Asian food centre).

Some migrants, especially Asians, are uncomfortable with the degree of freedom and free speech they find in Australia. They feel bombarded by brutal frankness, harassed by the sight of nudity and sex on television and in the cinema. In a way, they miss the firm framework of stricter rules and the soothing absence of moral choice. They are used to governments making decisions for them, like proxy parents. But suddenly, nobody cares what they do. So they feel uncared for—freedom too can create culture shock.

Another bummer, to use an Australian phrase, is the Australian pace of work, much slower than say, a Singaporean, a Hongkonger or an American might be used to. One former executive with a multi-national corporation, whom I know resigned in frustration from a civil service job, told me, 'I was going crazy, just twiddling my thumbs doing nothing all day. I had finished my work!' Needless to say, she wasn't very popular with her laid-back Aussie colleagues. Another rule—don't show off by working too hard if you want to be loved. Or work hard, but disguise it somehow.

More serious is the discovery on arrival, too late, that your professional qualifications are not valid in Australia. This is a very common problem, so do check carefully what you need to do to requalify for work in Australia, well before you arrive. Otherwise you will join the growing band of doctors, teachers and engineers running take-away food shops or struggling on student study grants.

Awful Things That Could Happen

You learn the hard way about certain basics of Australian life: if you forget to leave the rubbish bin out on the kerb for emptying on the appointed day (usually once a week only), too bad. After the third visit in a week from a door-to-door canvasser for charity, you learn to say 'No,' or ask them to send a letter instead.

You thought that swimming pool in the back garden a great idea, but now you find it costs a bomb to maintain in tip-top condition, the local Council has passed a rule on regular pool inspections (charging you an inspection fee for good measure) and any pools considered too accessible to children (your own or other people's) must be surrounded by an ugly isolation fence that will cost the earth to install.

You are terrified of your first winter after many years of living in the tropics, so you decide to order three tons of firewood in advance. Trouble is, there was no arrangement for when exactly it would be delivered. The wood arrives while you are out. It has been dumped in the back lane outside your garden fence, a good distance from your woodshed. You spend the next three days trudging back and forth with wheelbarrows and baskets to transport it all into the woodshed.

Yes, all this has happened to me.

Children Change

Luckily, however, I am not a parent. Migrant parents get upset when their children show signs of assimilating too well.

Singaporean friends of mine were typically protective Asian parents: they were driving their young son to and from school every day. But the boy soon asserted his new identity, demanding the same independence as his Australian schoolmates, who were all left to cycle to school by themselves. He didn't want to be seen as a sissy by his peers; he was going to be an Australian. The parents agonised for some time over road safety before giving way.

More serious identity problems may surface later. All that a migrant parent can do is be ready for these when they come, and perhaps just try to live with them.

Although such parents invariably will assure you that they migrated 'for the sake of the children', paradoxically they are filled with dread at the thought that their offspring may become loud, boorish and rebellious, or generally fall victim to sex, drugs and rock 'n' roll, as it were. Some kids do indeed react against their own background. That is a natural part of their adjustment process and must be accepted as such. The first symptom of mutation is the child's changing accent.

I witnessed an extreme teenage reaction to Malaysian roots. Gathering together for a home-cooked curry, the adults sat down with gusto to whack the goodies in time-honoured Malaysian fashion: with their fingers. When the family's daughter arrived home with her Australian friends, loud expressions of disgust were heard from her. The adults understandably told her to get lost. From the girl's point of view, she had been shamed before Aussie mates by her parents' primitive table manners, quite unacceptable to an Australian.

Yet I have also seen the Australian children of first-generation migrants cheering for their motherland's soccer team in matches against Australian teams. So you never can tell ...

Australian education in democracy and rights can make a parent's life perilous indeed. My Eurasian lawyer friend from Singapore got his comeuppance when he discovered that his Australian-born teen-age daughter had reported him to the local Human Rights and Equal Opportunity Commission for giving her a typical Asian 'tight slap' over some minor cheek the day before. She should have reported him to the local welfare authorities; but the incident did give him some pause for thought about brats' rights as he prepared his defence ...

Admirable environmental education in Australian schools can also produce annoying little home preachers, demanding you buy only dolphin-friendly, ozone-friendly and recycled-paper products.

On the Positive Side

It would be negligent not to warn you of the migrant blues. But there is a brighter side, some of which I hope will emerge in other sections of this book. Among the plus points are the exhilarating experience of freedom, space, and that special bright light that the Australian climate and geography produce. Enlightened attitudes to medicine, to education and to the environment abound. There is an easy friendliness on the streets and the peacefulness of daily life—and real, wild democracy. There is the excitement of a vast, largely wild land.

You may decide you like it all so much that you want to become an Australian citizen. Check on your own country's rules about dual citizenship (allowing it or not allowing it) before you take the plunge.

Having spent 24 non-consecutive months within your first five years in Australia, you are eligible to apply, and the letter confirming your citizenship can come as quickly as a surprising two weeks after you apply. The ceremony at which you receive your Certificate of Australian Citizenship, necessary before you can get an Australian passport (without which you cannot safely leave and re-enter Australia once you are an Australian national), could be a few more weeks. Here is one new citizen's account of the modest ceremony at which he received his citizenship, in Perth, Western Australia:

'We all trooped off to the Mayor's office, me and my two witnesses (you are not allowed more than two). On the seats in this room upstairs was a small package with our name tags on and a leaflet explaining our rights and duties as citizens. Altogether, our group of new citizens numbered 30.

'The Mayor's deputy made a speech and then they called us up in groups of about four or five to recite the oath of allegiance to Queen Elizabeth II (that probably won't go on much longer) and the country. … The Mayor shook our hands and gave us our certs, and also a little badge with the Aussie flag on it for us to wear. Then we posed with the Mayor for a photo if we wished, holding up our certs.

'Our local councillor made a speech: he said wasn't it wonderful how the Aussie World Cup soccer team was almost all migrant and how migrants introduced soccer and in such a short time took Australia to world standard, etc. Then we had some beers or sherry and what the Aussies call "finger food", and we all sang "Advance Australia Fair", and then went home.'

Chapter Five

DREAMTIME AUSTRALIA: THE ABORIGINALS

'There's nothing I would rather be
than to be an Aborigine
and dream of just what
Heaven
must be like
where moth and rust do
not corrupt
when I die I know I'll be
going up
'cos you know that I've
had my hell on earth—

Here I live in
this tin shack
Nothing here worth
coming back to
drunken fights and
awful sights
People drunk most
every night.
On the way to
a Bran Nu Dae
Everybody every body
say …'

—from *Bran Nu Dae*, an Aboriginal musical,
written by Jimmy Chi of Broome, Western Australia

If I begin simply by saying that this chapter is a minefield for the unfortunate author, you may get part of the picture.

There is no topic more sensitive in Australia—although the Anzacs and Gallipoli come a close second—than the Aboriginals. Approach the subject with caution; as I have said before, better shut up and listen, than put your foot in your mouth.

For a country as dedicated to the pursuit of democracy and human rights—and as critical of South Africa's track record—as Australia is, the 'Aboriginal problem' is a particularly painful Achilles heel. Every Australian, and every visitor, whether migrant or tourist, confronts 'the problem' sooner or later, and deals with it in his or her own way, sometimes with grace, but often with guilty resentment, or angry aggression.

Aboriginal children in Northern Territory outback. Photo by the author.

On the other hand, it is also very easy indeed to live in Australia without getting to know any Aboriginals, even without seeing any, particularly if you live in the larger cities. For many Australians, they remain but shadows on the fringes of life, phantoms that flit through the newspaper headlines.

For Americans conscious of their nation's lamentable track record with their own Indians, for white South Africans and for many others, Australia's problem is a case of *déjà vu*. Wherever we come from, we can probably conjure up other examples in the world which do not necessarily counterpoint only whites and non-whites; many a 'coloured' migrant race too has dominated another, weaker, similarly 'coloured' native race—in Southeast Asia and elsewhere.

What is 'the problem' in Australia? Basically, it is the spectacle of an underclass, which happens to be black, disadvantaged in almost every way, pushed to the fringes of society, so demoralised that it also seems to be bent on committing mass suicide in a variety of ways. And this in the midst of relative, white affluence.

They Came First

The Aboriginals themselves would prefer to be called names from their own languages: Koorie in the east and south (meaning 'Our People'), Nyunga in Western Australia, Yoingu in the Northern Territory, Anangu in central Australia and Nungga in South Australia.

These names, however, have not caught on to any great extent within white Australia, even less so in the world beyond Australia. For this reason, I am using the more conventional 'Aboriginal' in this chapter, with no insinuations attached.

'The First Australians' is the phrase most favoured among Australian liberals nowadays when referring to the original, black Australians, who may have come to Australia from Southeast Asia at least 40,000 years ago. Indeed, the Aboriginals' curly hair, blue-black skins, spread noses and thick lips are reminiscent of the peoples of southern India and Papua New Guinea. My Tamil husband is convinced they are fellow Tamils and prehistoric geography does make this conceivable. He is often approached in the street by Aboriginals as a 'brother'.

The term 'First Australians' serves to remind all Australians, whether migrant or of many generations' standing, that they are all newcomer settlers to some degree, compared with the Aboriginals. If you are a migrant 'new Australian', do not expect Aboriginal Australians to find common cause with you as a fellow minority, not even if you happen to be black.

For the Aboriginals, post-World War II migrant settlement of Australia has simply added to their woes, adding yet more human strata above them, further blurring their claim to real ownership of the country. Immigration has pinned them even more firmly at the bottom of the social pile.

Australia's most famous old-generation Aboriginal politician, lawyer and Martin Luther King-style freedom fighter, Charlie Perkins, Australia's first Aboriginal university graduate in 1965, expressed this feeling when he spoke out roundly condemning Asian immigration in the mid-1980s.

Statistical Phantoms

Aboriginals are thought to have numbered around 300,000–500,000, perhaps even more, when the Europeans arrived in Australia in 1788. The fact that their population had fallen to around 22,000 by 1860, as the European population zoomed above one million, speaks tragic volumes. But nobody really knows the true statistics, because Aboriginals were non-persons in census terms right up to 1967.

When the whites first arrived in Australia, they declared it an 'empty land', *Terra Nullius*, as if it were uninhabited. This was very convenient as it obviated the usual legal need to negotiate any kind of lease with traditional owners; the land could simply be taken. As writer John Pilger has put it in his *A Secret Country*, the Aboriginals were not accounted human but rather 'part of the fauna'.